C000184393

0
ides

Welcome to Oslo!

This opening fold-out contains a general map of Oslo to help you visualise the six districts discussed in this guide, and four pages of valuable information, handy tips and useful addresses. On the map, indicated by a star, are the ten sights not to be missed if your visit is short.

Discover Oslo through six districts and six maps

A Downtown East
B Downtown West
C Frogner / Bygdøy
D Majorstuen / Bislett / Blindern
E Grünerløkka / St Hanshaugen
F Grønland / Tøyen / Gamlebyen

For each district there is a double-page of addresses (restaurants – listed in ascending order of price – cafés, bars, tearooms, music venues and shops), followed by a fold-out map for the relevant area with the essential places to see (indicated on the map by a star ★). These places are by no means all that Oslo has to offer, but to us they are unmissable. The grid-referencing system (**A** B2) makes it easy for you to pinpoint addresses quickly on the map.

Transport and hotels in Oslo

The last fold-out consists of a transport map and four pages of practical information that include a selection of hotels.

Index

Lists all the street names, monuments and places to visit featured in this guide.

OUTDOOR OSLO

Oslo may be brimming with cultural events and places to eat and drink, but it is the city's natural surroundings that truly make it special. The Gulf Stream provides a mild climate – summer temperatures of 25–30°C (77–86°F) are not unusual – even though Norway lies far to the north. The country is a paradise for swimmers: the Nordmarka Forest has 343 lakes, while the Oslo Fjord boasts a 39-km (24-mile) shoreline, 40 islands and endless expanses of water to enjoy.

THE OSLO FJORD AND THE ISLANDS

December
→ Dec 10
The Nobel Peace Prize is presented at the town hall.

EATING OUT

Local eating habits
A hearty breakfast is followed by a light lunch around noon, and dinner as early as 4 or 5pm – so you have time to get hungry for a light evening meal around 9pm.

Restaurants
Opening hours
→ Usually noon–11pm
Reservations recommended at high-end restaurants. Many close for July and/or Aug.

What type of food?
In Oslo, food is generally of a high quality and there is a mix of culinary styles from all over the world. In a fishing nation like Norway, seafood is a reasonably priced choice.

Note that what is called a 'café' might well turn out to be a restaurant or a club.

Prices
Rather high, but there is a range to satisfy all budgets.

Tipping
Service is included (15%), but it is customary to leave a little extra.

BARS AND CLUBS

→ Bars and clubs downtown serve alcohol until 3am
Oslo has an active nightlife, with a number of bars, clubs, pubs, cafés and concert venues.

EXPLORING OSLO

On foot
Oslo City and Nature Walks
→ Tel. 41 31 87 40
oslowalks.no
Guided walks, including a thematic ghost walk, in the city and the surrounding forest.

By bus
H.M.K. Class (**B** C2)
→ Tel. 22 78 94 00
http://hmk.no/
Two- to four-hour coach tours of the city (in Norwegian, German and English; French and Spanish by reservation).

City Sightseeing
→ citysightseeing.no
Hop on from any one of the 18 stops throughout the city. The complete bus tour lasts 75 minutes.

By boat
Båtservice Sightseeing (**B** C5)
→ Rådhusbrygge 3
Tel. 23 35 68 90;
boatsightseeing.com
Hop-on hop-off Mini Cruise on a sail boat to/from the town hall, Opera or Bygdøy. It also offers a Grand Tour of Oslo (7½ hrs) and popular prawn cruises on the fjord.

By Land Rover
Kim Camp & Nordic Safari

THE ISLANDS

Hovedøya
→ Boat 94 from Vippetangen
A mere 400 yards of water and a public transport ticket separate you from this bathing paradise. The convent 'Cistercienserklosteret', which English friars began building in 1147, was pillaged and left in ruins in 1532.

Langøyene
→ As above
Oslo's former waste dump (until 1938) is now a jewel of the fjord.

NORDMARKA

Oslo is surrounded by untamed forests inhabited by bears, wolves, lynxes and 42 other mammal species, along with 1,200 plant varieties and 250 species of birds. The 430 sq. km (166 sq. miles) of forest are easily reached from the centre. For example, take metro line no. 1 to Frognerseteren, walk down to Sognsvann (2 hrs on foot, 1 hr on skis) and then take metro line 3 back to the city. Ullevålsseter, Tryvannsstua, Kikutstua, Kobberhaughytta and Skjennungstua are popular for meals and stopovers, while Sognsvann and Bogstadvannet are the top bathing sites.

The Norwegian Tourist Association
→ Tel. 40 00 18 68

AS Skiservice
→ Tel. 22 13 95 00; Sledges, skis and bicycles for hire

CITY PROFILE

- Norway's capital and largest city
- 586 860 inhabitants
- Over 3 million visitors in 2009
- More than 1,200 bars, cafés and restaurants
- Time zone: GMT + one hour
- Currency: the Norwegian krone (NOK)

ORIENTATION

- The Akerselva River draws a line between east and west
- Tallest buildings: the Plaza Hotel (117 m/ 383 ft) and Posthuset (111 m/364 ft)

KARL JOHANS GATE

FROGNER (VIGELAND) PARK

AKERSHUS CASTLE

WWW.

General information
→ visitoslo.com
→ visitnorway.com

Internet cafés
Arctic Internet Café (A D4)
→ Inside Oslo S
Tel. 22 17 19 40
Daily 9am–11pm
Mini business centre with 20 computers and Wi-Fi.

Qba (E C4)
→ Olaf Ryes plass 4
Tel. 90 55 34 34
Mon–Fri 8am–1am;
Sat-Sun 11am–1am
A pleasant café with three PCs and free Wi-Fi.

TOURIST INFO

Information centres (Turistinformasjon)
Town hall (Rådhuset)
(**B** D4)
→ Fritjof Nansens pl. 5, entry on Roald Amundsensg.
June-Aug: daily 9am–7pm;
April-May, Sep: Mon-Sat
9am–5pm; Oct-March:
Mon-Fri 9am–4pm
Trafikanten (A D4)
→ Jernbanetorget 1
Tel. 815 30 555; Mon-Fri 7am–8pm; Sat-Sun 8am– 6pm (8am–8pm May-Sep)

Telephone
To call Oslo from abroad
→ 00 (from the UK) + 47 (Norway) + eight-digit no.
To call abroad from Oslo
→ 00 + country code + the number you need
Emergency numbers
→ 110 (fire); 112 (police); 113 (ambulance)
Casualties (legevakt) (F A3)
→ Storg. 40
Tel. 22 93 22 93
Open 24 hours

DIARY OF EVENTS

March
Oslo Church Music Festival
→ Nine days; in various churches throughout the city

Holmenkollen FIS World Cup Nordic
→ Two days; mid-March
With ski jumping as a highlight.

May
Constitution day
→ May 17
Children's parade and downtown celebrations.

June
The Færder Regatta
→ Mid-June
Regatta from Aker Brygge to Horten via the Færder Lighthouse.
Oslo Medieval Festival (F B5)
→ Two days; in Middelalderparken
Knights' tournaments, jugglers, jesters, medieval songs and much more.
Holmenkollen Summer Concert
→ Mid-June
The Oslo Philharmonic at the Holmenkollen ski jump!
Norwegian Wood
→ Mid-June; four days

Family rock festival at Frognerbadet swimming pools.

July-August
Norway Cup
→ Late July
The world's largest youth football cup at Ekebergsletta (see **F**).
Øya-Festivalen
→ Early Aug
Big rock festival in the Medieval Park (see **F**).
Oslo Jazz Festival
→ Second week of Aug
Concerts, mostly traditional jazz, in the streets and in venues around the city.
Chamber Music Festival
→ Mid-Aug; throughout the city
International chamber music.

September-October
The ULTIMA Festival
→ Ten days, throughout the city
Contemporary music and theatre performances.

Welcome to Oslo!

A Downtown East
B Downtown West
C Frogner / Bygdøy

D Majorstuen / Bislett / Blindern
E Grünerløkka / St Hanshaugen
F Grønland / Tøyen / Gamlebyen

SLEMDAL

★ EMANUEL VIGELAND MUSEUM

TORGNY SEGERSTEDTS V.

SØRKEDALSVEIEN

VIGGO HANSTEENS VEI

ULLERNCHAUSSÉEN

SØRKEDALSVEIEN

MAJORSTUEN

KIRKEVEIEN

BOGSTADVEIEN

VIGELAND PARK

SKØYEN

★ OSLO CITY MUSEUM

KIRKEVEIEN

DRAMMENSVEIEN

HALVDAN SVARTES GATE

SJØLYSTVEIEN

FROGNER

PALACE PARK

NORWEGIAN FOLK MUSEUM ★

FROGNERSTRANDA

FROGNERKILEN

BYGDØY

KON-TIKI MUSEUM / FRAM MUSEUM ★

C

THE OSLOFJORD

LINDØYA

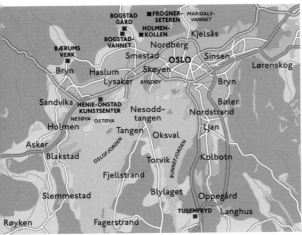

SLO AND THE SURROUNDING AREA

EXCURSIONS

Bogstad gård
➔ Sørkedalsv. 826
Tel. 22 06 52 00; May-Oct:
guided tours Tue-Sat 1pm
and 2pm; Sun 12.30, 1.30,
2.30 and 3.30pm
A beautiful 18th-century
manor and Norway's first
landscaped park; plus a
farm with animals the
children will love.

Henie–Onstad Kunstsenter
➔ Høvikodden, approx. 15
mins drive from Oslo (bus
lines 151, 161, 252 and 261)
Tel. 61 80 48 80; Tue- Sun
11am–7pm (5pm Sat-Sun)
Contemporary art in a
modern museum; plus a
magnificent restaurant
and beaches.

TusenFryd
➔ Vinterbro (by E18, 10
mins south of Oslo) Buses
from Bussterminalen
Tel. 64 97 64 97; Open at
the weekend May-Sep
(daily mid-June–mid-Aug);
call ahead for times
An amusement park
with rides that will leave
you legless. SpinSpider
puts you through 4.5Gs
at 115 km/h, Speed
Monster accelerates
from 0 to 90 kmph (55
mph) in two seconds.
MiniFryd for the very
young, SpaceShot and
BadeFryd if you want to
get wet.

Aurskog Hølands-banen (Tertitten)
➔ Train 460/riksvei 171
to Sørumsand; Tel. 63 86
81 50; July-Aug & Dec: Sun
11am, noon, 1, 2 and 3pm
For railway enthusiasts,
a 4-km (2 ½-mile) train
ride inside a traditional
carriage behind a coal
locomotive.

Summer

or snow-deprived visitors
slo does offer some
vonderful activities in
vinter. Summer, however,
an be a joy too, whether
laying golf, horseback
iding in the great
utdoors, swimming (see
rey box above left), even
aintball fighting and go-
art racing. For more
information go to the
ourist centres.

SHOPPING

Opening hours
➔ Mon-Fri 10am–5pm (6 or
pm Thu); Sat 11am–3pm
arger stores and shopping
nalls often stay open later

Department stores

Steen & Strøm (A C4)
➔ Kongens g. 23
Tel. 22 00 40 00

GlasMagasinet (A C3)
➔ Stortorvet 9
Tel. 22 90 87 00
Oslo's two classic

department stores.

Oslo City (A D3)
➔ Tel. 815 44 033; Mon-Sat
10am–10pm (8pm Sat)

Byporten (A D4)
➔ Tel. 23 36 20 20; Mon-Sat
10am–9pm (8pm Sat)
Two large shopping malls
by Jernbanetorget.

Aker Brygge (B B5-6)
➔ Tel. 22 83 26 80; Mon-Sat
10am–8pm (6pm Sat)
Seafront shopping area.

Eger Karl Johan (A B3)
➔ Karl Johans g. 23B
Mon-Sat 10am–7pm (6pm
Sat); egerkarljohan.no
High-end fashion in the
new, 9,000 sq.-metre
shopping centre by
Egertorget.

Bogstadveien (D D3-E4)
Shopping street filled with
designer fashion stores.

Crafts

Heimen Husflid (A B3)
➔ Rosenkrantz g. 8; Mon-Fri
10am–6pm; Sat 10am–3pm

Husfliden AS (A C3)
➔ Stortorvet 9 (Glas-

magasinet); Tel. 22 42 10 75;
Mon-Sat 10am–7pm (6pm
Sat)
Traditional sweaters and
other souvenirs.

Market

Youngstorget (A C-D3)
➔ Mon-Fri 9am–6pm
Fruit and vegetables.

OSLO FROM ABOVE

Summit 21 (B** D2)
➔ Scandinavia Hotel,
Holbergs g. 30
Tel. 23 29 3 00; Mon-Sat
4pm–1am (2.30am Fri-Sat);
Sun 5pm–1am
Classic bar-with-a-view –
even the loos have a
breathtaking outlook.

Sky Bar & Lounge (F** A4)
➔ Plaza Hotel,
Sonia Henies plass 3
Tel. 22 05 80 00
Mon-Thu 5pm–1am;
Fri-Sat 4pm–1.30am
Take a glass elevator to
reach the highest bar
in town.

HOLMENKOLLEN AND SKI MUSEUM

→ Kongev. 5
Tel. 22 29 42 30
A 15-minute walk from Holmenkollen metro station (Line 1)
June-Aug: daily 9am–8pm; (10am–4pm Oct-April; 10am–5pm May and Sep)
The stands of Oslo's landmark ski jump can hold up to 30,000 spectators – this is where the 2011 World Ski Championships will take place. The Ski Museum has a ski jump simulator, a shop, a café and an exhibition that relates 4,000 years of skiing history.

HOLMENKOLLEN SKI JUMP

OSLO PLAZA

PARADISBUKTA, BYGDØY

→ Ekebergv. 283
el. 22 29 42 30; kimcamp.no
dventure safari in the
rest, that also includes
iking, fishing, skiing,
anoeing, and more.

NTERTAINMENT

ickets
illettservice
→ Tel. 815 33 133
illettservice.no
ckets for sports events,
eatre plays, concerts etc.
phone or book online.
hat's on in Oslo?
monthly magazine
vailable from hotels and
urist centres.
lassical music
slo Konserthus (**B** C4)
→ Munkedamsv. 14
l. 23 11 31 00
he home of the Oslo
hilharmonic is also used
r larger family concerts.
en Norske Opera (**A** D3)
→ Kirsten Flagstads pl. 1
l. 21 42 21 21

An Olso landmark, the opera is housed in an award-winning building by the water. Take a tour, walk on the roof or watch a performance.
Rock and pop
Oslo Spektrum (**F** A4)
→ Sonja Henies pl. 2
Tel. 22 05 29 00;
oslospektrum.no
The vast arena can seat up to 10,000 people.
Rockefeller Complex (**A** D2)
→ Torgg. 16; Tel. 22 20 32 32
rockefeller.no
It comprises two medium-size music venues, Rockefeller Music Hall and John DEE Live Club & Pub, and a larger one across the street, Sentrum Scene.
Cinematheque
Filmens Hus (**A** C4)
→ Dronningens g. 16
Tel. 22 47 45 00 / 89
Screening of old classics and more recent films. Film museum (free entry).

MUSEUMS

Opening hours
→ Often closed Sun and/or Mon; opening times vary
Free entrance
To the national museums.
Discounts
Usually for children, senior citizens and students.

OUTDOOR ACTIVITES

Winter
Downhill skiing
→ Tryvann Winter Park (bus 41 to Årnes/metro line 1 to Voksenkollen, then ski bus); Tel. 40 46 27 00
14 runs (black to green), of which the longest is 1,400 m (1 ½ miles); terrain park with half-pipes, rails and jumps, seven lifts, ski instruction and cafés.
Ice-skating
→ Narvisen skating rink, Spikersuppa (**A** B3)
Tel. 95 70 95 05; Dec-March: daily 11am–9pm

→ Grünerhallen skating rink, Seilduksg. 30; Tel. 22 35 55 52
Oct-March: Sun noon–2pm
Skates to hire in both places.
Cross-country skiing
→ Info from Skiforeningen (Skiing Association); Tel. 22 92 32 00; skiforeningen.no; see also skiskole.com
2,600 km of prepared ski tracks just outside town. Skiing school with classes in slalom, telemark and snowboard.
Tobogganing
→ In Korketrekkeren; Metro line 1 to Frognerseteren (terminus); AS Skiservice (sleigh rental) at the bottom of the run, next to the Voksenkollen metro station; Tel. 22 13 95 00
The 1952 bobsleigh track has been turned into a 1.2 mile long toboggan run; it takes eight to 10 minutes to race down, 13 minutes to go back up by metro.

ASTRUP FEARNLEY MUSEUM OF MODERN ART

MUSEUM OF CONTEMPORARY ART

PIPERVIKA

Akershus-utstikker

Akershuskai, sondre

KONGENS GATE

KONGENS GATE

★ **NORWAY'S RESISTANCE MUSEUM**

★ **AKERSHUS CASTLE AND FORTRESS**

Festnings-plassen

★ **NORWEGIAN ARMED FORCES MUSEUM**

Vippetangkaia

5

6

0   150   300 m

A   **B**

MUSEUM OF CONTEMPORARY ★ ART

RIKSTEATRET

NORS ARKITEKT MUSE

Bankplass

MYNTGA

Grev

GLACIS

OPERATUN

Prinsessens plass

★ Akershus Castle and Fortress (A A5)

→ Tel. 23 09 39 17; Fortress: daily 6am–9pm; Castle: May-Aug: daily 10am (12.30pm Sun)–4pm, Sep-April: Sat-Sun noon–5pm; Guided tours: akershusslott.kontakt@mil.no

Oslo's impressive medieval fortress faces the waterfront. Begun by Håkon V in 1299, it was upgraded to an artillery fort in bastion fortress style from 1592, and used for military purposes until 1818. There's hardly a more peaceful spot for a stroll. Kings Haakon VII and Olav V rest in the castle church's mausoleum.

★ Norway's Resistance Museum (A A5)

→ Akershus Castle; Tel. 23 09 31 38; June-Aug: daily 10am (11am Sun)–5pm; Sep-May daily 10am–4pm (11am Sun)

Forty-two members of the resistance were executed at the fortress during World War 2. Historical artefacts, photographs and documents are on display under narrow 17th-century arches.

★ Norwegian Armed Forces Museum (A B6)

→ Akershus Castle, building 62; Tel. 23 09 35 82; May-Aug: daily 10am (11am Sat-Sun)–5pm; Sep-April: Tue-Sun 11am–4pm (5pm Sat-Sun)

A Spitfire and a German tank, dioramas and 80,000 books illustrate the armed forces' defence history since the Vikings.

★ Astrup Fearnley Museum of Modern Art (A C5)

→ Dronningens g. 4; Tel. 22 93 60 60; Wed-Sat noon–5pm

The Astrup Fearnley Museet for Moderne Kunst received attention after purchasing Jeff Koons' kitsch sculpture Michael Jackson and Bubbles. Other modern European and American artists on display include Francis Bacon, Anselm Kiefer, R.B. Kitaj, Damien Hirst. Also temporary exhibitions.

★ Museum of Contemporary Art (

→ Bankplassen 4; Tel. 21 20 00; Tue-Fri 11am–5pm (7pm Thu); Sat-Sun 12am

The Museet for samtidskunst focuses on post-1945 works, a most of the 3,000 piec are Norwegian. Also temporary exhibitions international art.

★ Kvadraturen (A B

After the great fire of left Oslo in ruins, Chri IV founded a new Renaissance city by th castle, Christiania. Lit it remains except for s buildings in its centre between Jernbanetor

A

Downtown East

Oslo Sentralstasjon, or Oslo S, is the busiest entrance to Norway's capital city and is situated in the older and less glamorous part of the downtown area. However, this urban jungle hides several treasures. Between Karl Johans gate, and Akershus Castle, historic brick houses from Christian IV's city of 1624 have been taken over by museums and upscale restaurants. Linking Stortorvet with Youngstorget, Torggata is lined with shops, whereas from Youngstorget until Grünerløkka to the north (see E), it's one kebab shop after another. Luxury is transforming Akersgata, once the home of Oslo's newspapers.

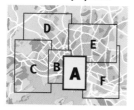

SOLSIDEN

TRATTORIA CAPPUCCINO

RESTAURANTS

Hai Café (A D2)
→ Calmeyers g. 6
Tel. 22 20 38 72
Mon-Sat 11am–10pm;
Sun noon–10pm
The hidden treasure of Oslo's Chinatown serves reasonably priced, tasty Vietnamese dishes. Try the nearby Saigons Lille Café, Møllergata 32. Main courses NOK 60–149.

Hell's Kitchen (A C2)
→ Møllerg. 23
Tel. 22 11 20 00
Daily 2pm–3am
Diner-inspired eatery by Youngstorget, serving one of the city's best pizzas. Pizza NOK 120.

Arakataka (A D2)
→ Mariboes g. 7
Tel. 23 32 83 00; Daily 4pm–10pm (11pm Fri-Sat)
Creative, French-inspired gourmet food at unbeatable prices.
Carte NOK 159–179.

Solsiden (A A5)
→ Søndre Akershuskai 34
Tel. 22 33 36 30; May-Sep
Outdoor summer restaurant serving inventive seafood dishes such as roast turbot with lobster sauce. The house speciality is the large seafood platter (minimum two persons) at NOK 635 per person.

Statholdergaarden (A B4)
→ Rådhusg. 11
Tel. 22 41 88 00
Mon-Sat 6pm–midnight
Sumptuous yet intimate 18th-century baroque interiors in which Bocuse d'Or champion Bent Stiansen creates new four- to six-course menus daily, always based on seasonal produce. The best petits fours in the city. Relaxed yet professional service. Carte NOK 390.

CAFÉS, ICE CREAM PARLOUR

Dolcevita (A B4)
→ Prinsens g. 22
Tel. 22 42 23 36; Mon-Sat 7.30am (10am Sat)–8pm; Sun 11am–6pm
Italian confectionery shop with delectable ice cream, sandwiches and Neapolitan coffee. One ice cream scoop NOK 25.

Trattoria Cappuccino (A C3)
→ Domkirkeparken
Tel. 23 35 70 65; Mon-Sat 11am–10pm; Sun 1–10pm
The sun glitters off the steel tables in this leafy green oasis between ancient arcades and Oslo Cathedral. Snack meals NOK 110–225.

NORWEGIAN ARMED FORCES MUSEUM

NORWAY'S RESISTANCE MUSEUM

AKERSHUS CASTLE AND FORTRESS

KAFÉ CELSIUS

BARE JAZZ

FESTMAGASINET STANDARD

Kafé Celsius (A B4)
→ Rådhusg. 19
Tel. 22 42 45 39; Daily
11am–midnight (10pm Sun)
Popular courtyard tables
in summer, and cosy
open fires in winter.
The building was once
a residence for Oslo's
mayors.

Kaffistova (A B3)
→ Rosenkrantz' g. 8
Tel. 23 21 41 00; Daily
11am–9pm (7pm Sat-Sun)
Traditional wholesome
cooking – tried and
tested favourites such as
sour cream porridge, liver
in cream sauce, cod,
whale beef and
dumplings – all served
with soft drinks, true to
temperance traditions.

BARS

Biblioteksbaren (A B2)
→ Bristol, Kristian IVs g. 7
Tel. 22 82 60 00 Mon–Thu
4–11.30pm, Fri–Sat 10am–
1.30am, Sun 11am–11pm
A classic hotel bar with
Chesterfield furniture and
shelves of books giving a
library atmosphere. An
oasis of peace in the
midst of the city's bustle.
Coffee and Braastad
VSOP NOK 110.

London Pub (A B2)
→ C.J. Hambros plass 5
Tel. 22 70 87 00

Daily 3pm–3.30am
The slightly worn-out
main gathering spot of
the gay community.
Jukebox and billiards in
the basement, Gloria
Gaynor-disco on the
ground floor. Karaoke
every Tuesday and bingo
on Thursday.

CONCERTS, CLUBS

Herr Nilsen (A B2)
→ C.J. Hambros pl. 5
Tel. 22 33 54 05; Daily 2pm–
3am; herrnilsen.no
Intimate concert venue
featuring live jazz, folk
music and blues. Adult
crowd.

Café Mono (A D3)
→ Pløensg. 4
Tel. 22 41 41 66 ; Mon-Sat
11am–3am; Sun 6pm–3am;
cafemono.no
Classic rock club. Daytime
café/diner with live music
at night. Rock musicians
of all generations are
among the guests. Beer
NOK 52.

Garage (A C3)
→ Grensen 9
Tel. 22 42 37 44; Mon-Sat
1pm–3.30am; Sun from
6pm; garageoslo.no
Rock club and café with
a large backyard and
frequent basement gigs
ranging from hard rock to
pop and metal.

SHOPPING

Record shops
Downtown East houses
many small record shops
where you can find a
reasonably priced
souvenir.

Tiger Safari (A D3)
→ Hammersborgg. 18
Tel. 22 20 73 50; Mon-Fri
noon–6pm; Sat 11am–5pm
Punk, emo and hardcore,
hip hop and indie.

Big Dipper (A D2)
→ Torgg. 16
Tel. 22 20 14 41; Mon-Sat
11am–6pm (4pm Sat)
Rock, indie, pop, 60s,
reggae, electronica and
more, on vinyl and CD.

Bare Jazz (A C3)
→ Grensen 8; Tel. 22 33 20
80; Mon-Sat 10am–6pm
(midnight Wed-Sat)
Everything jazz, with
knowledgable staff and a
relaxing courtyard café.

**Kunstnerforbundet
(A** A3)
→ Kjeld Stubs g. 3
Tel. 23 31 02 40; Tue-Sat
11am–5pm (6pm Thu; 4pm
Sat); Sun noon–4pm
Graphic art, paintings
and sculptures to suit all
budgets, made by 250
Norwegian artists.

**Festmagasinet
Standard (A** B4)
→ Prinsens g. 25
Tel. 22 42 96 40; Mon-Tue

10am– 5.30pm; Wed-Fri
9.30am– 5.30pm (6.30pm
Thu); Sat 10am–6pm
Whoopee-cushions,
gorilla suits and jokes for
all ages makes even a
rainy holiday fun.

Heimen Husflid (A B3)
→ Rosenkrantz' g. 8; Tel. 23
21 42 00; Mon-Sat 10am–
5pm (6pm Thu; 3pm Sat)
National costumes and
local crafts in tin, wood
and textiles, amongst
other traditional
souvenirs.

Moods of Norway (A B3)
→ Akersg. 8
Tel. 46 62 77 96; Mon-Sat
10am–7pm (6pm Sat)
The big barn door,
between the Louis
Vuitton and Burberry
shops, hides the latest
Norwegian fashion hit.
Fun, edgy fashion for
men and women.

Posthallen (A C4)
→ Prinsens g. 10
Tel. 48 30 06 00
Mon-Sat 10am–5pm (6pm
Thu; 3pm Sat)
Oslo's old main post
office houses a small
number of great stores:
Flashdance offers 80s
vintage glam and
Freudian Kicks carries a
mix of designer labels.
Sheltered backyard with
Italian gourmet food
among Arabic columns.

▼ Map F

PARLIAMENT

KVADRATUREN – CHRISTIANIA SQUARE

▼ Map E

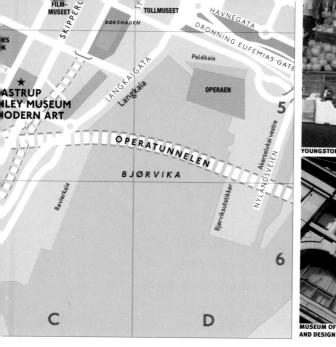

YOUNGSTORGET

MUSEUM OF DECORATIVE ARTS
AND DESIGN

...orget and
...husfestning.
...strict is known
...e Kvadraturen, or
...rangle, because of its
...gular street pattern.
...torget, a statue of
...ian IV himself points
...ere the city was to be
The area contains a
...er of museums.

...liament (A B3)
...l Johans g. 22
...d tours: Sat 10 and
...m, 1pm; arrive 15mins
...; Groups: 9.45am and
...m, by appt (tel. 23 31 31
...omviser@stortinget.no)
...tortinget, in yellow
...nd red granite, was
...rom 1861–66 by the

Swede Emil V Langlet. In
the assembly hall, the
parliament representatives
can draw inspiration from
Oscar Wergeland's
painting, *The Founding
Fathers at Eidsvoll*.

**★ Oslo Cathedral and
Kirkeristen (A** C3)
→ *Stortorget 1 Tel 23 62 90 10
Mon-Fri 10am–4pm; Fri 3pm–
8am (Sat); Sat 10am–4pm;
Sun 10am–7pm*
The altarpiece and pulpit
(1699), the English steeple
clock (1718) and E.
Vigeland's stained-glass
paintings (1916) are among
the highlights of Oslo's
main church, where crown
prince Haakon and Mette-

Marit wed in 2001. Behind
the church, eateries and
craft stores now occupy
Kirkeristen, the old neo-
Romanesque arcaded
butcher's stalls built by
Christian H. Grosch in
1840–59.

★ Youngstorget (A D3)
Home of the labour
movement and starting
point for large rallies and
May Day demonstrations,
Youngstorget Square was
constructed as a produce
market in 1846. Today, the
anthem *The Internationale* is
used to signal the last call
in the eponymous café by
the Opera Passage. On the
opposite side lies the old

arcade of vending stalls
(1876–7). Up a staircase,
between the slightly
worn arcades, are some
pleasant cafés.
**★ Museum of
Decorative Arts and
Design (A** B–C1)
→ *St Olavs g. 1 Tel. 22 03 65 40
Tue-Fri 11am–5pm (7pm Thu);
Sat-Sun noon–4pm*
The Kunstindustrimuseet
houses Norwegian and
foreign crafts, fashion and
design from the 7th century
to the present day. Of note
is the unique Baldishol
tapestry from the 12th-
century, silver, ceramics,
East Asian objects and
royal costumes.

AKER BRYGGE

NOBEL PEACE CENTRE

MUNKEDAMSVEIEN

5

Bryggetorget

Filipstadkaia

Olav Selvaags
plass

6

TJUVHOLMEN
★

0   150   300 m

A   B

★ **Royal Palace /
Palace Park** (B B-C 2-3)
→ *Henrik Ibsens g. 1; Tours in
English Mon-Thu, Sat noon,
2 and 2.20pm; Fri, Sun 2,
2.20 and 4pm; NOK 95;
Tickets from billettservice.no*
The majestic trees, English-
style rolling green lawns
and idyllic ponds are all
you need for a walk in the
country... in the city. The
park was designed by royal
gardener Mortensen and
palace architect Linstow
(1825–48). Originally, the
Empire-style royal palace
was to be built on Tøyen,
but King Karl Johan (on
horseback on the front
grounds) wanted it here.

★ **Ibsen Museum** (B B3)
*Henrik Ibsens g. 26; Tel. 22 12
35 50; Tue-Sun 11am–6pm
(4pm mid-Sep–mid-May);
Tours every hour on the hour*
The museum is located in
the house where the
playwright lived from 1895
until his death in 1906. It is
restored to its original style
and offers a revealing
glimpse into his life.
Changing exhibitions.

★ **Stenersen
Museum** (B C4)
→ *Munkedamsv. 15 (access
via Konserthusterrassen)
Tel. 23 49 36 00; Daily 11am–
7pm (5pm Wed, Fri-Sun)*
Rolf Nesch, Ludvig Karsten,
Jacob Weidemann, Kai

Fjell, Edvard Munch and
other Norwegian artists
from the 1850s to the
1970s. Painting and
photography exhibitions.
★ **Aker Brygge** (B B-C5) /
Tjuvholmen (B B6)
→ *Tel. 22 83 26 80*
The wharf in Pipervika
brims with tourists and
locals each summer. In
1982 the shipyard Akers
Mek. Verksted gave way to
a development of
restaurants, shops, offices,
luxury dwellings and a
marina. The modern
designs in glass and steel
co-exist happily with the
tastefully restored
industrial buildings,

making it one of the m
architecturally pleasin
parts of Oslo.
★ **Nobel Peace
Centre** (B C5)
→ *Tel. 23 46 16 00; June
15: daily 10am–7pm; Se
May: Tue-Sun 10am–6p*
War, peace and confli
negotiations are the f
of the Nobels Fredsse
with information abou
Nobel Peace Prize lau
★ **Town Hall / Town
plaza** (B C–D5)
→ *Tel. 23 46 16 00; Dail
6pm; Free tours Mon, W
10am, noon and 2pm*
The monumental Råd
was completed by
Modernists Arnstein

IBSEN MUSEUM

ROYAL PALACE

Map labels:

4

NASJONAL-
BIBLIOTEKET

THOM

SOLLIGATA

CORT ADELER

HANSTEEN

PARKVEIEN

GATE

RUSELØKKA

IBSEN

IND.-EKS.-
HUSET

Løpsetorvet
(Solli plass)

HENRIK IBSENS GATE

SOMMERROGATA

HYDROPARKEN

BYGDØY ALLÉ

INKOGNITOGATA

OSCARS GATE

FROGNERVEIEN

DRONNINGPARKEN

INKOGNITO
TERRASSE

BEHRENS GATE

COLBJØRNSENS GATE

3

PARKVEIEN

DRONNINGDAMMEN

KONGES

PARK

RIDDERVOLDS GATE

SKOVVEIEN

MELTZERS GATE

NIELS JUELS GATE

INKOGNITOGATA

OSCARS GATE

Riddervolds
plass

CAMILLA COLLETTS VEI

LALLAKROKEN

PRESIDENT HARBITZ GATE

2

URANIEN-
BORG

SKOVVEIEN

HAREBAKKEN

BRISKEBYVEIEN

SUNDTS

ELLERT

URANIENBORG

JOSEFINES GATE

Nordahl
Rolfsens
plass

HOLTES GATA

HOMAN

URANIENBORG

JOSEFINES GATE

BRISKEBY

URANIENBORG-
PARKEN

JØRGEN MOES GATA

DAAS GATE

URANIENBORGVEIEN

HOLTEGATA

DAAS GT.

INDUSTRIGATA

1

LANGAARDS-
LØKKEN

PROF. DAHLS GATE

B

A

STENERSEN

All the symbols that define a nation are located around Studenterlunden: the parliament, the National Theater, the university and the royal palace. On May 17th – Constitution Day – residents and tourists alike gather on Karl Johan to see the children's parade. The rest of the year, the area will seduce you with its variety of shops, bars, cinemas, theatres and restaurants. Head north for a stroll in the Palace Park, or south to Aker Brygge and Tjuvholmen. Here you can gaze at the modern architecture, enjoy the busy harbour life, or linger over a drink and a good meal on a bright summer's evening.

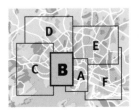

THEATERCAFEEN

PALACE GRILL

RESTAURANTS

Santinos (B D4)
→ Tordenskiolds g. 8–10
Tel. 22 41 16 22
Mon-Fri 11am (Sat 1pm)–
11pm; Sun 2–10pm
A busy place with
a large selection of
authentic Italian dishes.
Carte NOK 119–198.

Dinner (B D4)
→ Stortingsg. 22
Tel. 23 10 04 66
Daily 11am–11pm
Have your pick of spicy
Szechuan or Cantonese
gourmet dishes. Popular,
so book ahead. Carte
NOK 134–269.

Theatercafeen (B D4)
→ Stortingsg. 24
Tel. 22 82 40 50; Mon-Sat
11am–11pm; Sun 3pm–10pm
Elegant, continental
cuisine in classic
Viennese Jugendstil
surroundings. However,
it is the legendary mix of
high society and bohemia
that draws people here.
Carte NOK 235–335.

**Lofoten
Fiskerestaurant (B** B6)
→ Stranden 75, Aker Brygge
Tel. 22 83 08 08; Mon-Sat
11am–1am; Sun noon–10pm
Wonderful
mediterranean-inspired
seafood dishes, varying
with the seasons – shell-
fish in summer,

traditional 'lutefisk' in
autumn and spawning
cod in the new year.
Expensive food, but the
cheapest beer in the area
at the bar. Carte NOK
274–298.

Palace Grill (B A4)
→ Sollig. 2; Tel. 23 13 11 40
Daily 5pm–3am (midnight
Sun-Mon)
The small, gourmet
restaurant section of
Palace Bar. The menu
changes daily, depending
on ingredients and the
chef's mood. You can't
book, so get there early.
Ten courses NOK 1025–
1080 (or negotiate a
menu with fewer courses).

CAFÉS, BARS, CLUBS

**Pascal konditori
og brasserie (B** C4)
→ Henrik Ibsens g. 10
Tel. 22 55 00 20
Mon-Sat 9am (10am Sat)–
11pm; Sun noon–5pm
The best French
patisserie in town serves
delicious brasserie food
in the evening.

Beach Club (B B5)
→ Bryggetorget 14; Tel. 22
83 83 82; Mon-Fri 11am–
10pm (11pm Wed-Fri); Sat-
Sun noon–11pm (7pm Sun)
This American-style café
has been a staple ever

LORRY

NORWAY DESIGNS

since Aker Brygge opened in 1989. The generous-sized Beach Burgers are popular with the locals.

Ferja (B D5)
→ Rådhusbrygge 1
Tel. 22 42 43 12; May-Aug: daily 2 (1pm Sat-Sun)–11pm
The boat is moored at the town hall pier every summer. More relaxed, and cheaper beer than in Aker Brygge.

Lorry (B C2)
→ Parkv. 12; Tel. 22 69 69 04
Mon-Sat 11am–3pm; Sun noon–1.30am
A traditional establishment that displays arts and crafts made by some of its regulars – a mixed crowd of artists, actors and musicians. Decent food and a wide range of beers.

Lekter'n (B C5)
→ Stranden 3
Tel. 21 02 36 21; Daily 11–3am (depending on weather)
At Aker Brygge's floating restaurant, huge beach umbrellas provide shade for the elegant lounge bar with soft chairs. Popular with a young crowd. A summer staple in Oslo.

Palace Bar (B A4)
→ Sollig. 2; Tel. 23 13 11 40
Daily 3pm–3.30am
A classic bar playing country rock and live concerts on Monday

nights, patronised by the wealthy crowd of west Oslo. The courtyard bar, Skaugum, is artistically decorated with sinks and pictures of Elvis.

Kunstnernes Hus Bar og Restaurant (B C2)
→ Wergelandsv. 17
Tel. 22 69 44 22; Tue-Thu noon–1pm; Fri-Sat noon–3am; Sun noon–6pm
The airy, minimalist vestibule of the Kunstnernes Hus art gallery, by the Palace Park, serves as a hangout for Oslo's cultural elite. Simple, tasty gourmet fare.

Onkel Donald (B D4)
→ Universitetsg. 26
Tel. 23 35 63 10; Daily 11am–midnight (3am Fri-Sat)
Roomy, quiet place with books and magazines, games nights, food and a free meeting room for business clients is available. At weekends the pace picks up.

SHOPPING

Norway Designs (B C4)
→ Stortingsg. 28
Tel. 23 11 45 10
Mon-Fri 9am–5pm (7pm Thu); Sat 10am–4pm
Stationery, glassware, clothing, quilts, watches and more in Norwegian and international design.

Tronsmo bøker og tegneserier (B D3)
→ Kristian Augusts g. 19
Tel. 22 99 03 99
Mon-Fri 9am–5pm (6pm Thu-Fri); Sat 10am–4pm
Independent bookshop free of knick-knacks and toys, but with a huge section of comic books (mostly Norwegian and English) downstairs. Quality books guaranteed.

Nomaden (B B2)
→ Uranienborgv. 4
Tel. 23 13 14 15; Mon-Sat 10am–6pm (4pm Sat)
Daydream amongst a myriad of maps, mosquito nets, backpacks and every conceivable form of travel literature.

Åpent bakeri (B A3)
→ Inkognito terrasse 1
Tel. 22 44 94 70; Mon-Fri 7.30am–5pm; Sat 8am–3pm
The delicious bread here takes five to six hours to bake, and marginally shorter to buy – but it's worth enduring the queues.

Indre Oslofjord Fiskarlag (B C5)
→ Rådhusbrygge 3 and 4
Tel. 22 42 02 75
Tue-Sat from 7am
The fishermen's co-op sells fresh Oslo Fjord shrimps at NOK 60–90/l.

Get there early in the morning for the catch of the day.

House of Oslo (B B4)
→ Ruseløkkv. 26; Tel. 23 23 85 60; Mon-Sat 10am–8pm (6pm Sat); houseofoslo.no
A shopping mall in Vika with some 20 shops specialising in design and interiors, including the first Illums Bolighus store outside Denmark.

Sadoni Couture (B B2)
→ Uranienborgv. 7a
Tel. 22 46 41 54; Mon-Fri 9am–4pm (3pm Thu); Sat 11am–2pm by appt
Wedding dresses designed by Trude and Hamid Sadoni, who also make exclusive evening gowns.

Kamikaze Men / Kamikaze Donna (B B1)
→ Hegdehaugsv. 24 and 27
Tel. 22 60 20 25/22 59 38 45
Mon-Sat 10am–5pm (7pm Thu; 5.30pm Fri; 3pm Sat)
Step into designer heaven with labels such as Prada, Gucci, YSL, Paul Smith and classics by Cerruti. Astronomically expensive!

Sprell leker (B B1)
→ Hegdehaugsv. 36
Tel. 23 22 22 22
Mon-Fri 10am–6pm
Educational toys for children, nursing corner and baby care room.

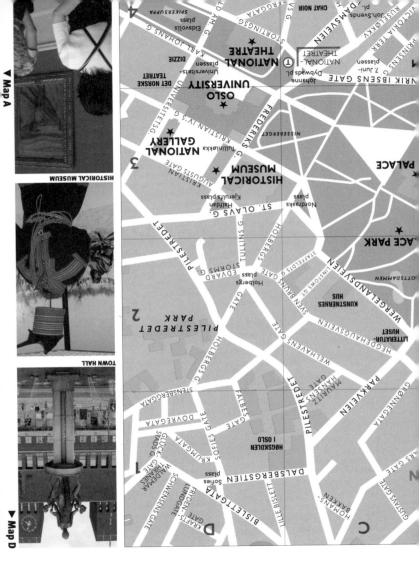

▼ Map A

HISTORICAL MUSEUM

TOWN HALL

▼ Map D

OSLO UNIVERSITY

DET NORSKE TEATRET

NATIONAL THEATRE

CHAT NOIR

DIZZIE

KARL JOHANS G.

SPIKERSUPPA

Eidsvolls plass

BERGGATA

STORTINGSG.

JOH. SVENDS G.

VICTORIA TERRASSE

PRINSENS GATE

NATIONAL THEATRET

Dybwads plass

Johanne Dybwads pl.

7. Juni plassen

HENRIK IBSENS GATE

Universitets- plassen

NATIONAL MUSEUM

NATIONAL GALLERY

Tullinløkka

FREDERIKS G.

UNIVERSITETSG.

KRISTIAN IV'S G.

NISSEBERGET

HISTORICAL MUSEUM

KRISTIAN AUGUSTS GATE

ST. OLAVS G.

Halfdan Kjerulfs plass

Nordraaks plass

PALACE

PACE PARK

OTTSDAMMEN

PILESTREDET

HOLBERGS G.

TULLINS G.

EDVARD STORMS G.

STREELDS G.

Holbergs plass

PILESTREDET PARK 2

SVEN BRUNS GATE

WERGELANDSVEIEN

KUNSTNERNES HUS

LITTERATUR- HUSET

HEGDEHAUGSVEIEN

WELHAVENS GATE

MARITZ HANSENS GATE

PILESTREDET

PARKVEIEN

GRØNNEGATA

STENSBERGGATA

HOLBERGS G.

FALBES GATE

KRUMGATA

SOFIES GATE

DOVREGATA

HØGSKOLEN I OSLO

Sofies plass

DALSBERGSTIEN

BISLETTGATA

GLÜCKSTADS G.

WALDEMAR THRANES GATE

KRAFTS GATE

FRIDTJOFS GATE

LUNDGATA

SCHWENSENS GATE

FRIDTJOFS GATE

LILLE BISLETT

HOMANS- BAKKEN

GUSTAVS GATE

GS GATE

OSLO UNIVERSITY

NATIONAL THEATRE

...berg and Magnus ...sson for the city's ...year celebrations in ... Every year, the Nobel ...e Prize is awarded here.

...storical ...eum (B D3)
→ *ederiks gate 2*
2 85 99 12; May 15-Sep
...e-Sun 10am–5pm; Sep
...y: Tue-Sun 11am–4pm
...e museums in one:
...niversity Museum
...tiquities displays
...e-Age tools and rock
...ngs, Bronze-Age
...llery and weapons,
...eval church art, and
...orld's best preserved
...g helmet. The
...ographical Museum

has a unique Netsilik-Inuit collection, with 900 items from Roald Amundsen's Gjøa expedition. The Mint Collection holds Norway's oldest bank note, issued in Bergen in 1695.

★ National Gallery (B D3)
→ *Universitetsg. 13*
Tel. 22 20 03 41; Mon, Wed,
Fri 10am–6pm (7pm Thu);
Sat-Sun 11am–5pm
The Scream and other famous paintings by Munch, *Bridal procession in Hardanger* by Tidemand and Gude, and National Romantic works by JC Dahl, Fearnley and Tidemand are among the highlights in the country's largest

collection of pre-1945 Norwegian and international art. It also houses fine collections of French Impressionism and Russian icons, and the best art library in the country.

★ Oslo University (Faculty of Law) (B D3)
→ *Karl Johan's g. 47*
Tel. 22 85 95 55
Oslo University, or Universitas Osloensis, was founded by Frederik VI in 1811. The buildings, by architect Christian H. Grosch and the German master architect Schinkel, date from 1854. Edvard Munch's giant frescos, in the Great Hall, behind

Domus Media, are currently closed to the public.

★ National Theatre (B D4)
→ *Johanne Dybwads*
plass 1; Tel. 22 00 14 00
The baroque-style Nationaltheatret, by Henrik Bull, was completed in 1899 despite strong protests from the university. The interior is rococo with a touch of Art Nouveau. The main stage (752 seats), the Amfi stage (212 seats), the Malersalen (60 seats) and the satellite Torshovteatret all focus on classical drama. The international biennial Ibsen Festival is held here in August.

VIGELAND MUSEUM

OSCARSHALL

BYGDØY

OSCARSHALL ★

OSCARSHALLVEIEN

MUSEUMSVEIEN

DRONNINGHAVNVEIEN

STRØMSBORGVEIEN

GOL STAVKIRKE

5

NORWEGIAN FOLK MUSEUM

MELLBYEDALEN

HUK TERRASSE

MUSEUMSVN

HUK AVENY

LANGVIKSVEIEN

Festplassen

VIKING SHIP MUSEUM ★

FREDRIKSBORG CHRISTIAN BENNECHES VEI

LANGVIKSBUKTA

KON MU

TERRASSE

BYGDØY HAMAR JORANS VEI

BYGDØY KAPELLVEI

HUK AVENY

6

BYGDØY

LANGVIKSVEIEN

FREDRIKSBORGVEIEN

BYGDØYNESVEIEN

LØCHENVEIEN

BYGDØYNESVEIE

NOR MARITI

FREDRIKSBORGVEIEN

A

ADMIRAL BØRRESENS V. **SJØMANNSKIRKEN**

B

★ **Vigeland Park (Frognerparken)** (**C** B-C1)
→ *Open daily, all year*
Oslo's second largest park, and a popular recreational area for the locals.

★ **Vigeland Sculpture Park** (**C** B-C1)
→ *Main entrance on Kirkeveien; Tel. 23 49 37 00 (museum info)*
Norway's main attraction, with one million visitors a year. Gustav Vigeland (1869–1943) spent years planning and realising his Monolith, the Wheel of Life, the large wrought-iron gates on Kirkeveien and the 200 other sculptures scattered around the park.

★ **Oslo City Museum** (**C** C2)
→ *Frogner Hovedgård, Frognerv. 67; Tel. 23 28 41 70 Tue-Sun 11am–4pm (5pm July-Aug); July-Aug: guided tours in English, Sat 2.30pm*
In the Frogner manor house (1790) portraits, artefacts and photographs tell Oslo's history of cultural, urban and industrial development over a thousand years. Norwegian interiors from 1750–1900 are also displayed here.

★ **Vigeland Museum** (**C** C2)
→ *Nobels g. 32 Tel. 23 49 37 00; Daily 10am–5pm (noon–4pm in Sep-May)*

The artist's former studio, an award-winning building in neoclassical style (1923) by Ree and Buch, now houses the Vigelandmuseet. It contains some original full-size plaster casts of Vigeland's sculptures and his woodworks. His apartment on the third floor has been left unchanged since the sculptor died in 1943 (his ashes are in the tower room). In summer, concerts are held in the courtyard (Sun).

★ **Oscarshall** (**C** B4)
→ *Oscarshallv. Tel. 91 70 23 61*

May-Sep: Sat-Sun 11am– (Wed-Mon June 15-Aug 15 tours every hour, on the h The romantic silhouett behind the masts of the yachts in Frognerkilen Oscar I's summer pala built in 1847–52 in a n Gothic style and decor by Tidemand and Gude

★ **Viking Ship Museum** (**C** A5-6)
→ *Huk aveny 35 Tel. 22 13 52 80; Daily 9a 6pm (10am–4pm in Oct-* On display are three o best-preserved Viking ships in the world, bui oak in the 9th century. Oseberg ship is the be preserved, and the on

C

VIGELAND'S SCULPTURE PARK

VIGELAND PARK

C

Frogner / Bygdøy

Oslo's most exclusive residential area lies between the Palace Park, the open spaces of the Vigeland Park and the yachts in Frognerkilen. Stylish 1890s apartment blocks alternate with mansions along its broad streets of majestic trees and impressive facades. When the chestnut trees bloom on Bygdøy Allé, it is time to embark on a journey to Bygdøy, the 'Museum Island'. In Bygdøy, you can admire the king's horses, stroll in the woods or study Norwegian maritime history and Norwegian culture – old culture in Folkemuseet or modern culture at Oslo's most popular beaches: Huk, Paradisbukta and 'Homolulu'!

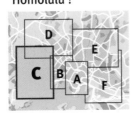

BØLGEN & MOI

LE CANARD

RESTAURANTS

Pizza da Mimmo (**C** D3)
→ Behrens g. 2 (access on Skoveien); Tel. 22 44 40 20
Daily 4–11pm (10pm Sun)
Italian pizza and red wine served on rustic tables in a cosy basement. Many claim this is the best pizza in town, so it is wise to book ahead.
Pizza NOK 105–135.

Mares (**C** D3)
→ Frognerveien 12 B
Tel. 22 54 89 80
Restaurant: Mon-Sat 11am–3pm (4pm Sat), 5pm–12.30am;
Wine bar: 11.30am–3pm, 5pm–midnight
Fish and shellfish are important natural resources in Norway, and there aren't many who can cook them as well as chef Lucien Mares, who boldly pairs the fish with veal and lamb. The wine list is magnificent. Main course NOK 225–265.

Lille Herbern
(south of **C** B6)
→ Bygdøy
Tel. 22 44 97 00
Bus no. 30 to Herbernveien; walk to the end of the road; a ferry (NOK 30) will take you to the restaurant. Open summer only: Mon-Fri 4.30–10pm (also noon–4.30pm mid-June-Aug); Sat-Sun

noon–10pm
Norway's shortest ferry-ride (every half hour) is the only way to get to the tiny island, Herbern. You'll be hard pressed to find a more romantic spot, even though the menu is limited. Snack dishes for lunch; main course NOK 169–190.

Bølgen & Moi Briskeby (**C** D2)
→ Løvenskiolds gate 26
Tel. 24 11 53 53
Mon-Sat 7.30 (9am Sat)–1am; Sun 11am–5pm
The old power station in Briskeby is the setting for this popular eatery. At street level is the bar and breakfast hall with an open fire, long tables, and an elegant brasserie serving high-quality traditional dishes; upstairs the mezzanine serves up an elaborate, gourmet French-Italian cuisine with a Norwegian twist. Main course NOK 225–360.

Le Canard (**C** D3)
→ President Harbitz' g. 4
Tel. 22 54 34 00
Mon-Sat 6–10pm
Michelin star-restaurant situated in an elegant 1899 brick villa. Enjoy a glass of champagne on the patio before you enter the grand dining hall.

ODEN STRANDRESTAURANT

FROGNERPARKENS CAFÉ

CARPE DIEM

Excellent gourmet food, and a wine cellar that has been awarded Wine Spectator's Award of Excellence. Three-course menu NOK 695.

CAFÉS

Hukodden Strandrestaurant
(south of **C** B5)
→ *Huk beach, Bygdøy Badebåten ('bathing boat') from Rådhusbrygge 3*
(**B** D5); *Tel. 22 43 74 62 Daily noon–10pm (Sat-Sun only in autumn)*
Take in the delightful view of the sea from perhaps the prettiest beach in Oslo. There's room for 250 outside and 50 inside Quisling's old bathhouse. Main course NOK 175–195.

Frognerparkens Café / Herregårdskroen (**C** C2)
→ *Frognerveien 67 Tel. 22 43 77 30 Daily 10am–midnight (depending on the weather)*
The two open-air restaurants next to Frogner Hovedgård are musts for enjoying the first outdoor beer of the spring. Herregårdskroen is more intimate, snugly sheltered under large green trees, while Frognerparken Café

enjoys more sun. Both offer a selection of snack dishes, a small selection of main courses and beer, of course, from NOK 66.

BARS, CLUB

La Belle Sole (**C** D3)
→ *Observatorieg. 2B Tel. 22 55 40 00 Thu-Sat 11pm–3am; Wed cocktail bar*
Intimate, exclusive club in a Jugendstil building by Solli plass, where the young and glam have been dancing for years. Dress code, no-one under 26 and stiff prices ensure an exclusive clientèle.

Champagneria (**C** D3)
→ *Frognerveien 2; Tel. 21 94 88 02; Mon-Thu 4pm–1am (2am Wed; 3am Thu); Fri 3pm–3am; Sat 1pm–3am*
All kinds of sparkling wine at a wide range of prices (a glass of cava is only NOK 34). Tapas (from NOK 39) to counter the effect of the bubbles. For NOK 150, you can blind test one cava and two champagne brands.

Enoteca Vinbar (**C** C3)
→ *Bygdøy Allé 59 C Tel. 23 27 09 27; Mon-Sat 11.30–1am; Sun 4–9pm*
An intimate wine bar that also serves snacks and an inexpensive dinner.

SHOPPING

Skovveien (**C** D3)
This street, up to Riddervolds plass, is lined with exclusive fashion stores.

Hassan og Den Dama
→ *Skovv. 4; Tel. 22 55 30 99*
Here you will find items by the Danish SamsøeSamsøe, Norwegian Tho, Odd Molly, Valerie, Juicy Couture, and a large selection of designer jeans, shoes and accessories.

Benedicte Ferner
→ *Skovv. 12; Tel. 24 11 90 22*
Elegant garments by Vivienne Westwood, Paul & Joe, DKNY, See by Chloé and others.

Carpe Diem
→ *Skovv. 7; Tel. 22 44 80 10*
Light, romantic clothes and accessories for women, plus must-haves for the home. In the tiny Fresh next door (Skovv. 8), you will find elegant, Nordic fashion from So Hee, Ivana Helsinki and Soaked in Luxury.

Det søte liv
→ *Skovv. 27; Tel. 22 44 24 00*
Exclusive lace lingerie from Italy and France.

Briskebyveien (**C** D2–3)
Three minutes' walk from Skovveien, you can buy

Simen Sæthre's cakes, coffee at Mocca and yet more clothes:

Ma
→ *Briskebyv. 28 Tel. 22 60 72 90*
Avant-garde, slightly androgynous women's clothing by Ann Demeulemeester, Costume National, Rick Owen, Miu Miu, Balenciaga and others. Next door, Lille Ma Vintage sells second-hand designer items.

Secret Society
→ *Briskebyv. 38 (access on Lallakroken)*
Hidden-away store, run by self-proclaimed 'clothes nerds' with a talent for discovering new brands. Alexander Wang, Comme des Garçons, Thumori Chisato, Junya Watanabe, Visvim shoes and Lara Bohinc jewellery and accessories.

Face it (**C** D3)
→ *Frognerv. 13 Tel. 22 56 22 70 Mon–Fri 9am–7pm (5pm Fri); Sat 10am–4pm*
In Frogner, appearances tend to matter. Laser treatment, massage, peeling, pedicures, manicures and a range of therapies are on offer to make sure you look your best in your expensive clothes.

NORWEGIAN FOLK MUSEUM

VIKING SHIP MUSEUM

▼ Map B

▼ Map D

Map (right side labels):

OBSERVATORIE TERRASSE

SKILLEBEKK

DRAMMENSVEIEN

SKILLEBEKK

4

GABELS GATE

JULES GATE

NASJONAL-
BIBLIOTEKET

MOGENS
THORSENS
PARK

FREDERIK STANGS GATE

SOPHUS LIES GATE

HEFTYES GATE

OSTRUP TERR.

SIMLE

HYDRO-
PARKEN

Løpsetorvet (Søul plass)
Observatoriegata

RØDE KORS
KLINIK

MOGENS THORSENS GATE

GATO

FRITZNERS

THOMAS

TOSTRUPS GATE

SKOV VEIEN

FROGNERVEIEN

OSCARS GATE

BYGDØY ALLÉ

AM. LUTH.
CHURCH

FROGNER

GIMLE
TERRASSE

SKALGSSONSGA

N-B-

GIMLE

COLBJØRN-
SENS GATE

BERGENS GATE

NIELS JUELS GATE

HAXTHAUSENS GATE

KRUSES GATE

Little ROGNER ALLÉ

ELISENBERGVEIEN

LØVENSKIOLDS

ANTM. FURUS
plass

ODINS GATE

GÜLLEVEIEN

MAGNUS
BERGS GATE

THOMAS HEFTYES GATE

3

GYLDENLØVES GATE

NIELS JUELS GATE

HARBITZ GATE

BRISKEVEIEN

Grabo Bergs
plass

EILERT
SUNDS GATE

NORDRAAKS

TIDEMANDS GATE

ECKSBERGS GATE

ODINS GATE

ECKSBERGSVEIEN

FROGNER

GATA
LINDEMANS
GATE

FROGNER
TERRASSE

Solheims
plass

2

SCHIVES GATE

BRISKEBY

BRISKEBYVEIEN

BALCHENS GATE

GYLDENLØVES GATE

SIGNS
GATE

LANGGARDS GATE

Frogner
plass

ATE

INDUSTRIGATA

LANGAARDS
LØKKEN

MUNTHES GATE

Amaldus
Nielsens pl.

FROGNER-

OSLO
CITY MUSEUM

★

FUGLEHAUGGATE

FJERNKUGT

FROGNER-

1

MAJORSTUEN

ST.
DOMINIKUS

NEUBERGGATA

JACOB AALLS GATE

PROF. DAHLS GATE

ELTERS GATE

KIRKEVEIEN

MARIES GATE

SINNTAGGEN

DAMMENE

PARK

ENEN

SUNDSVEIEN

MAJORSTUEN

VALKYRIEGATA

ESSENDROPS GATE

BOGSTADVEIEN

ADOLF
GATE

GATE

SØRKEDALSVEIEN

MIDDELTHUNS GATE

KIRKEVEIEN

MIDDELTHUNS FABRIKKVEI

LANDSPARKEN

D

C

LAHELLEHOLOEN

GJESTEHAVN

NGEN

FILIPSTADVEIEN

Hjortneskaia

Brannskjærutstikker

FILIPSTAD

5

Filipstadutstikker

AM MUSEUM

NES

OSLOFJORDEN

6

1

0   100   200 m

C   D

NORWEGIAN
MARITIME MUSEUM

FRAM MUSEUM

earing a dragon's
rom the Viking era.
ips and their owners
laced in burial
ds to facilitate their
y to the afterworld.
male skeletons were
scovered in the
ls along with grave
including sledges,
, boxes and textiles.

wegian
Museum (C A5)
eumsv. 10; Tel. 22 12
Mid-May–mid-Sep:
am–6pm; otherwise
pm (4pm Sat-Sun)
ve church (13th
) is the oldest of the
ldings that make up
ormous outdoor

Norsk Folkemuseum. In
summer there's traditional
cooking, folk-dancing,
livestock displays and
guided tours. Children can
buy old-fashioned sweets
and play with vintage toys.
Christmas fair in Nov/Dec.

★ **Kon-Tiki**
Museum (C B6)
→ Bygdøynesv. 36; Tel. 23 08
67 67; June-Aug: daily
9.30am–5.30pm; April-May,
Sep 10am–5pm (4pm March);
Nov-Dec 10.30am–3.30pm
The museum holds the
original eponymous balsa
raft in which Thor Heyerdahl
(1914–2002) sailed from
Peru to Polynesia in 1947. It
also contains the straw

boat Ra II from 1970, a
model of the Tigris, statues
from Easter Island, and a
10m-long shark-whale.

★ **Norwegian Maritime**
Museum (C B6)
→ Bygdøynesv. 37; Tel. 24 11
41 50; Mid-May–Aug: daily
10am–6pm; Sep–mid-May
daily 10am–4pm (Thu 6pm)
Norway has a long
coastline and arable land
is scarce, so the sea has
been a natural area in
which to make a living.
Here you can see
Norwegian coastal culture
and maritime history, in the
shape of maps, models,
navigation equipment,
more than 20 boats, the

polar ship Gjøa and the
schooner Svanen.

★ **Fram Museum (C** C6)
→ Bygdøynesv. 36
Tel. 23 28 29 50; Daily, June-
Aug: 9am–6pm; May, Sep:
10am–5pm; March-April, Oct
10am–4pm; Nov-Feb 10am–
3pm (4pm Sat-Sun)
The schooner Fram, custom
built in Larvik by Colin
Archer for Fritjof Nansen,
was used in three major
polar expeditions. The last
was Roald Amundsen's
South Pole expedition in
1911. The ship's interiors
paint a vivid picture of
what life was like for the
explorers trapped in the
polar regions for years.

Map (top)

VIGELANDSPARKEN

DELTHUNS GATE ESSENDROPS G

MONOLITTEN

★
FROGNER STADIU
AND SKATING MUSE

DEN ENGELSKE
PARK

FONTENEN

FROGNER-
BADET

"SINNATAGGEN"

ARNSTEIN ARNEBERGS VEI

JONSRUDVEIEN

FROGNER-

KIRKEVEIEN

PROF. DAH

GUSTAV VIGELANDS VEI

HYLLVEIEN

MADSERUD
TENNISANLEGG

4

0   100   200 m

MADSERUD ALLE

FUGLEHAUGGATA

MUNTHES GATE

A   B   C

INTERNATIONAL MUSEUM OF CHILDREN'S ART

EMANUEL VIGELAND MUSEUM

NRK ENTERTAINME

★ Bislett Stadium (D F4)

→ *Bislettg. 1 Tel. 23 46 20 00*
Norway's internationally
famous Bislett Stadium
won a special place in
Oslo's heart as a skating
rink and home ground for
Vålerenga F.C. and the
national football team,
which played Sweden here
in 1913. Later came the
clubhouse and grandstand
(1922), the Functionalist
style buildings (1940), the
European Championship,
the World Championship,
the Olympic Games, 55
track sports world records
(and 14 on skates), decay,
demolition and a 2004–6
redevelopment.

★ Villas in Homansbyen (D E4)

The Homan brothers
purchased land around
Josefines gate and Oscars
gate in 1853. G.A. Bull
designed the first villas
and set the standard for
later architects. Thus, the
architecture in Homansbyen
is unusually uniform, even
though the villas each
have an individual finish.
The finest is probably at
Josefines gate 13 (1860,
G.A. Bull), and has a
round corner tower.

★ Frogner Stadium / Skating Museum (D C4)

→ *Middelthunsg. 26; Tel. 22
43 49 20; Skating Museum:
Tue–Thu 10am–2.30pm;
Sun 10am–2pm; NOK 20*
The statues depicting
skating world champions
Oscar Mathisen (A.
Durban, 1959) and Sonja
Henie (Per Ung, 1986)
outside the 1912 Frogner
Stadion remind you of the
glory days when it was the
world centre of skating
sports. The Skøytemuseet
(Skating Museum) displays
prizes, skates and other
artefacts from 1850 to the
present day.

★ Football Museum (north of D F1)

→ *Ullevål stadium, Sognsv. 75
Tel. 23 00 83 07; Mon–Fri
10am–6.30pm (3.30pm*
Mon); Sat–Sun 11am–5p.
tickets from the Fotballs
NOK 80 (NOK 50 for chil
NOK 200 for families)
The dream of playing f
the national team is
embodied in the
Fotballmuseet, situate
the grandstand of the
national team's stadio
Here, 'Drillo', Norway'
legendary coach of th
1990s, amongst othe
worshipped as a hero

★ Tramway Museum (D D3)

→ *Vognhall 5, Gardev. ⋯
Tel. 22 60 94 09
Sat–Mon noon–3pm*
In 1894, Oslo became
first Nordic city to hav

D

Map labels (top to bottom, area names and streets):

VOLVAT · KAPELL · VESTRE GRAVLUND · THAULOWS VEI · TÅRNVEIEN · SØRKEDAL...

FRØEN (T) · DIAKONIVEIEN · VOLVAT MED. SENTER · VESTRE KREMATORIUM · BORGEN (T)

GUDBERGS VEI · SVENSENVEIEN · SKØYENVEIEN · HEGGELIVEIEN · PALIVEIE... · LILLE FR...

INTERNATIO... MUSEUM O... CHILDREN'S ★

DIAKONHJEMMET

FABRITIUSALLEEN · REIDAR KOBRO... · HARTVIG HALVORSENS VEI · BORGENVEIEN · BORGENBAKKEN · LILLE BORGEN · THODORE DAHLS VEI · BORGENVEIEN

SØRKEDALSVEIEN · TUENGEN ALLE · SVALBARDVEIEN · HJØRUNGVEIEN · HEGGELIBAKKEN · MUNKENGVEIEN

BORGEN · CHARLOTTE ANDERSENS VEI · TUENGEN ALLE

HAFSLUNDVEIEN · HAAKON DEN GODES VEI · SLEMDALSVEIEN · ANNE MAR... · KVERNST... · IVAR AASENS VEI · DAMKER... · TURNVEIT · SOGNSVANN

STEINERUD (T)

VINDEREN · RASMUS WINDERENS V. · VAR AASENS VEI · HAAKON DEN GODES VEI · BORGENVEIEN · JACOB HANSENS VEI · TUENGEN ALLE

FOSS... · SEBR... · PSYKI... KLIN... · LYDER... · VINES V...

TORGNY SEGERSTEDTS VEI · SOLSKINNSVN. · GRIMELUNDSHAUGEN · LØNNHAUGEN ALLE · BISKOP ...NDS V · GRIMELI... · DALSVEIEN

VINDEREN (T)

EMANUEL VIGELAND MUSEUM ★

C   B   A

FROGNER STADIUM AND NORWEGIAN SKATIN...
STIFTET 18-2-1864

VILLAS IN HOMANSBYEN

BISLETT STADIUM
BISLETT STADION

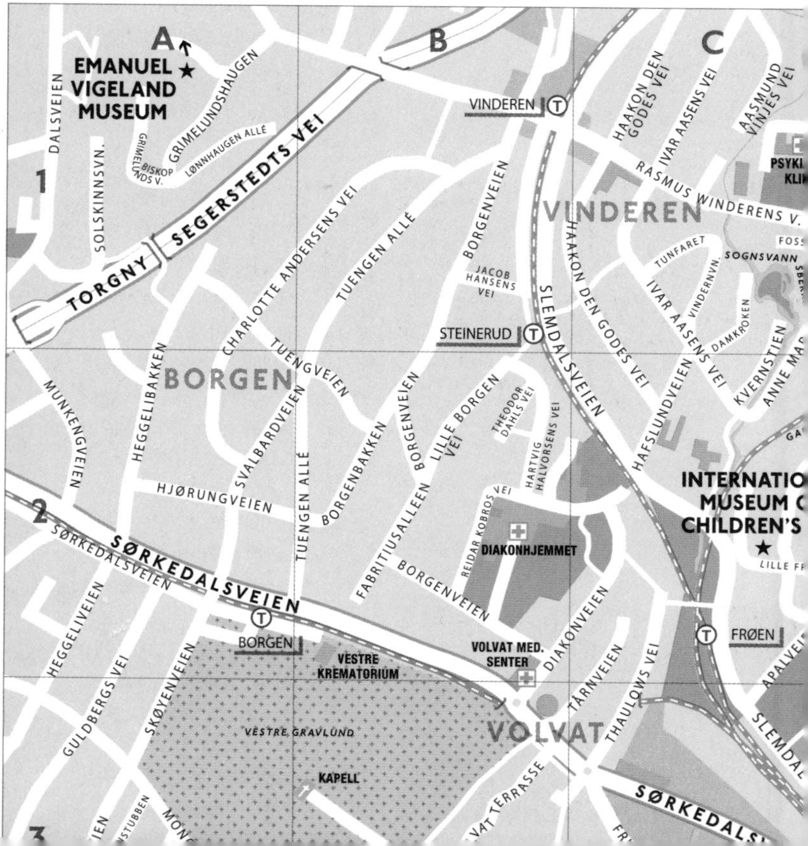

In the heart of Oslo's West End, Majorstuen is a well-appointed, interesting neighbourhood, where the metro station acts as the starting point for most activities, be it a visit to the best cinema in town (Colosseum), the prettiest park (Frognerparken) or the most exclusive shopping streets (Bogstadveien and Hegdehaugsveien), the latter of which will lead you all the way down to the Palace Park. The famous Bislett Stadium lies close by, next to the old Frydenlund brewery, which has been turned into Oslo's college centre. The university campus at Blindern is just two more stops on the metro.

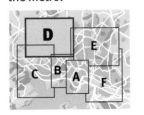

CURRY & KETCHUP

BOLIVAR

RESTAURANTS

Krishna's Cuisine (D C3)
→ Sørkedalsveien 10B
Tel. 22 69 22 69
Mon–Sat 11am–8pm (7pm Sat)
Tasty, cheap and healthy vegetarian food by Colosseum cinema. The daily special is often a rice casserole with papadums and soup. Herbal tea and root coffee accompanies the food. Daily special NOK 125.

Curry & Ketchup (D D3)
→ Kirkev. 51
Tel. 22 69 05 22
Daily 2–11pm
Indian tea and rice bags are stored along the walls of this casual restaurant. Students and backpackers tuck into chicken tikka masala and lamb curry accompanied by Indian – or Irish – folk music. Main course NOK 90–120.

Bambus (D D3)
→ Kirkev. 57
Tel. 22 85 07 00
Daily 2–11pm (midnight Thu–Sat; 10pm Sun–Mon)
Clean, sun-yellow eatery and bar with cheerful staff, which successfully masters such varied cuisine as Thai, Vietnamese, Chinese and Japanese. The kung pow (scampi, scallops and crab with cashew nuts) is strongly recommended. Main course NOK 169–278 (cheaper weekdays 2–6pm).

Cru vin & kjøkken (D E4)
→ Industrig. 50
Tel. 23 98 98 98
Mon–Sat 4pm–midnight
An intimate restaurant and wine bar downstairs with comfortable leather sofas and a welcoming fireplace. Nordic Master Chef Kari Innerå produces tempting dishes. There is an extensive wine list. Main course NOK 220.

Nodee (D C3)
→ Middelthuns g. 25A
Tel. 22 93 34 50
Mon–Sat 11am–11pm;
Sun 3–10pm; May–mid-Sep: daily 11am–9.30pm (Sun 10pm)
The Far East meets the affluent west side clientèle at the popular Nodee, known for excellent sushi and dishes such as braised spare ribs with kumquat and soy sauce. In the summer season you can sit outside. Asian menu NOK 545; Zen menu NOK 685.

RS & CO

KRISTINES FRANSKE FRISTELSER

PUR NORSK

CAFÉS

Café M (D D3)
→ Valkyrieg. 9
Tel. 22 60 34 00
Mon-Sat 11am–1am;
Sun noon–midnight
With several outdoor
tables pitched in the
middle of the shopping
crowd, Café M is a
meeting spot for local
residents who are not
put off by the expensive
beer (NOK 58, 0,4l).

Bolivar (D E4)
→ Vibes g. 11
Tel. 22 46 71 00; Mon-Sat
1am–11pm (midnight Thu-
Sat); Sun noon–8pm
Stylish, trendy café,
serving cheap, delicious
food made daily on the
premises. Interior shop
in the basement selling
French bedding, South
African tableware and
antique marble dishes
from the Netherlands.
Soup of the day NOK 89.

BARS, CONCERTS

**Chateau Neuf and
Betong (D** C3)
→ Slemdalsv. 7
Tel. 22 84 45 11
studentersamfundet.no
This students' concrete
colossus hosts everything
from rock festivals and
theatre performances, to
house parties and
political debates. Betong
is the basement club.

**Oslo
Mikrobryggeri (D** E4)
→ Bogstadv. 6 (entry on
Holteg.); Tel. 22 56 97 76
Daily 3pm (noon Sat)–1am
Oslo's only surviving
brewery has been serving
its own beers – from pale
lager to dark stout –
since 1989.

Horgans (D C2)
→ Hegdehaugsv. 7
Tel. 22 60 87 87
Mon-Fri 4pm–midnight
(3.30am Thu-Fri); Sat noon–
3.30am; Sun 2–10pm
Feel the energy levels at
this well-established
American-style sports
bar. A dynamic crowd fill
the dance floor, tasty
hamburgers too.

SHOPPING

**Bogstadveien
(D** D3-E4)
→ bogstadveien.no
Norway's longest, busiest
shopping street has
become younger and
more dominated by
chains, but all the big
brands are still here.

Georg Nilsen Fisk & Vilt
→ Bogstadveien 39
Tel. 22 46 50 16; Mon-Sat
9am–5pm (3pm Sat)
A delicatessen where the
fourth generation of
Nilsen sells antelope, elk,
alligator, reindeer, bear,
shellfish and fish.

Lille vinkel sko (D E3)
→ Kirkev. 59
Tel. 22 46 86 18; Mon-Fri
9am–7pm; Sat 10am–5pm
This independent store
sells the latest fashion
in shoes, for men and
women, including some
Norwegian designers.

Voga (D E4)
→ Professor Dahls g. 5
Tel. 22 69 07 60; Mon-Sat
10am–6pm (4pm Sat)
Fashion for those who
want to be noticed.
Dsquared2 and Vivienne
Westwood brands draw
celebrities here.

Oliviers & Co (D E4)
→ Dronning Astrids g. 7
Tel. 22 56 57 52
Mon-Fri 10am–6pm
(7pm Thu; 5pm Sat)
Exclusive oils and treats
from the Mediterranean.

Obelisque (D F4)
→ Dronning Astrids g. 7
Tel. 22 60 19 34; Tue-Fri
noon–5pm; Sat 11am–2pm
Functionalist, Art Deco
and Jugendstil lamps.

**Tonica Vintage
Corner (D** D3)
→ Schønings g. 14
Tel. 22 60 22 06
Tue-Sat 11am–5pm
Oslo's most famous
vintage store caught the
trend early – Tone Sige
started selling used
designer clothes in 1976.
1970s creations by
Chanel and Dior – and
even one of Jackie
Kennedy's sparkly tops
was for sale here.

**Kristines franske
fristelser (D** E3)
→ Kirkev. 98
Tel. 22 69 90 11; Tue-Fri
7am–5.30pm; Sat-Sun
8.30am (10am Sun)–4pm
Gorgeous, tempting
cakes made by French
pastry chef Alain Jean-
Joseph, and sold by the
cheerful Kristine.

Pur norsk (D F3)
→ Tereses gate 14
Tel. 22 46 40 45; Mon-Fri
11am–6pm; Sat 10am–4pm
Shop here for the very
best in Norwegian design.
Chairs, lamps, kitchen
utensils and lots more.

Chicas & venner (D D4)
→ Jacob Aalls gate 13
Tel. 22 606 606
Mon-Sat 10am–6pm
(7pm Thu; 5pm Sat)
Beautiful home furniture
– from tables and
wardrobes to mirrors and
china – mostly in wood
painted white, cream,
grey or black; also
women's clothing with a
vintage, rustic-style look,
by Odd Molly and
ChillNorway.

▼ Map E

STENSGATA
ADAM-
STUEN
GEN. BIRCHS GATE
VALLEFEKKA
IDIOTEN

BRAGEVEIEN
BAGGERRÜG

GÖRGGTA
WOLFES GATE
PILESTREDET
JACOB AALLS GATE
SUHM

KEYVEIEN
HARALD HARFAGRES
GARDEVEIEN
GYDAS VEI
MAJORSTUEN
AMMWAY
USEM

NORGES
VETNINÄRHGG-
SKOLE
OLE JACOB
BROCKS GATE
SOGNSVN.
THULSTRUPS GATE
Sophus
Buggs
plass
GABEITZ
GATE
AUGUSTE
CAPPELENS
GATE
SCHWIGS
GATE
RAINS

ULLEVÄLSVEIEN
WILHELM FÆRDENS VEI
SOHMSGATE
SUHMSGATE

Bjørnsterne
Bjørnsons
plass
MARIENLYST

STENSGATA
SOGNSVEIEN
KIRKEVEIEN

ULLEVÄLSVEIEN
NRK ENTERTAINMENT
CENTRE ★

Halvor
SEMI SKLANDS
Blinderens
plass
SEM
SÆLANDS
VEI

VESTRE AKER †
BLINDERNVEIEN

BLINDERN
PRESTEGÅRDSVEIEN
PETT TOLLERS

ULLEVÄL
SYKEHUS ✚

OSLO UNIVERSITY
– BLINDERN ★

NEDRE
ULLEVÄL
SOGNSVEIEN
HASSELBAKKEN
HASSEL-
HAUGVEIEN
MOLTKE MOES VEI
DUELIANG

ULLEVÄL
ULLEVÄLSALLÉEN
TERRASSE
HERBERGG
Arvid
Storsveens
plass
CHRISTOPHER
HANSTEENS VEI

John
Colletts
plass

ULLEVÄL
HAGEBY

PROBLEMVEIEN
APATVEIEN

Ⓣ BLINDERN

ADALLÉEN

TURNV.
EGTV.
HEB.E.
SOGNSVEIEN
VÄLVEIEN
VÄSKELADPVEIEN
NIELS HENRIK ABELS VEI

ULLEVÄLSALLÉEN
JOHN
COLLETTS
ALLÉ
HJORTEN
EIGENS VEI
Lars
Ramstads
plass
EVENTRYVEIEN
VESTGRENSA
VESTGRENSA

FOOTBALL
MUSEUM ↓

JUTULVEIEN
Dampliassen

VESLEFRIKK
VEIEN
TRIHANS-
VEIEN
Ⓣ FORSKNINGS-
PARKEN

E
D

FOOTBALL MUSEUM
TRAM MUSEUM

UNIVERSITY LIBRARY

OSLO UNIVERSITY IN BLINDERN

...ic trams, (later ...med 'trikker'). ...orveismuseet has ...toric tram carts – and ...veteran tramway ...mer.

...nuel Vigeland ...um (north of **D** A1)
→ ...elundsv. 8 (metro line ...ndal); Tel. 22 14 57 88 ...n–4pm (5pm May-Sep)
...r eyes adjust to the ...this dimly-lit ...leum, you will be ...nelmed by the erotic ...sco – 800 square ...of writhing male ...male bodies ...ng human life from ...tion to death.
...Vigeland's deeply

religious younger brother (1875–1948) is considered a pioneer in modern fresco painting.

★ **International Museum of Children's Art** (**D** C2)
→ Lille Frøens v. 4; Tel. 22 46 85 73; Tue-Thu 9.30am–2pm; Sun 11am–4pm
The Barnekunstmuseet, which opened in 1986, has paintings and objects made by children from all over the world, music sessions, storytelling and activities.

★ **NRK Entertainment Centre** (**D** E2)
→ Glassgården, Bjørnstjerne Bjørnsons pl. 1, Marienlyst

Tel. 23 04 25 20; Daily 9am (11am Sat-Sun)– 4pm; NOK 80 (children NOK 50); guided tours Sat–Sun 1pm (NOK 140/ 90/family NOK 370)
In the NRK's (Norwegian Broadcasting Corporation) Opplevelsessenter you can read the weather or the news, be a sports commentator or radio theatre actor. Interesting props and costumes on the guided tours.

★ **Oslo University – Blindern** (**D** D–E 1–2)
→ Administrasjonsbygningen (9th floor) Problemv. 7, Blindern; Tel 22 85 50 50
The majority of Oslo University's 36,000

students and 3,200 scientific staff members, are based in Blindern. The area was reserved for the university in 1923. Within two years the dormitory was built, and natural sciences moved here in the 1930s. Historians, social scientists and mathematicians followed in the 1960s. The new university library, built in the Modernist style, with a huge glass façade and massive columns, was inaugurated in 1999, and holds five million books. The Frederikke cafeteria is a good place for a budget meal, including halal food.

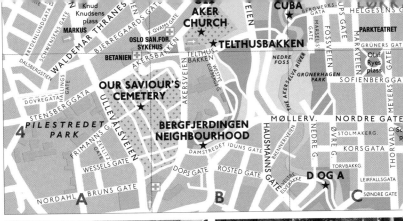

TELTHUSBAKKEN

BIRKELUNDEN PARK

★ **Akerselva** (E D1-C4)

The Akerselva River runs from Maridalsvannet to Bjørvika (**F** A5), dividing the city into east and west. Akerselva Miljøpark, a broad belt of paths that follow the river for 8 kms (5 miles) from Vaterland to its source, makes a very pleasant excursion, by foot or bike. Twenty-nine bridges cross the river: the *Norse Sagas* mention one situated where the Grüner Bridge is today, and the Anker Bridge is decorated with sculptures (1937) by Dyre Vaa. The 54-meter-long iron-suspension Åmot Bridge was moved here

from Telemark. There was early waterpower development in this area and the first grain mill (1341) was located at Sandaker. A new era began in the 1840s with the textile and mechanical industries. The mills of the industrial age have now been converted into offices, and the river is clean again.

★ **Bergfjerdingen neighbourhood** (E B4)

→ *Fredensborgveien, Dops gate and Damstredet*
Originally a ramshackle shantytown for the poor, where, in 1833, the cholera epidemic killed every sixth

inhabitant. In 1839, the newly-wed Henrik Wergeland moved into the ground floor of Damstredet Many artists still live in the picturesque wooden buildings, the oldest of which date from the 18th century.

★ **Our Saviour's Cemetery** (E A-B3)

→ *Akersbakken 32, entrance on Ullevålsveien*
A walk through Norwegian history. Vår Frelsers Gravlund (1808) was the only cemetery in Oslo until 1833. The 'cemetery of honour', in the centre, dates from 1903; this is where cultural icons like

Ibsen and Munch, the statesman C.J. Hambro others important Norw figures are buried.

★ **Old Aker Church** (I
→ *Akersbakken 26; Tel. 2 91 20; Tue, Fri noon–2pr* Oslo's oldest preserve building, Gamle Aker K dates from the 11th ce and is made of Roman and has three naves. T baroque-style pulpit a font were designed by Thomas Blix in 1715. Th steeple is from 1861.

★ **St Hanshaugen** (E
→ *By Ullevålsveien*
In the 1840s people er huge Midsummer Eve bonfires on this moun

E

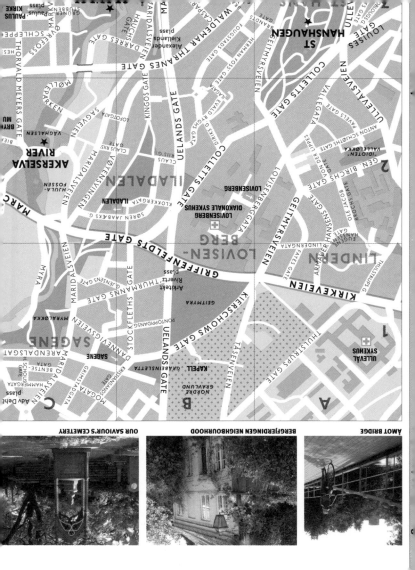

ÅMOT BRIDGE

BERGFJERDINGEN NEIGHBOURHOOD

OUR SAVIOUR'S CEMETERY

Grünerløkka is a 15-minute walk away from Karl Johan: an 'urban village' with colourful, square 19th-century city blocks, numerous bars and cafés, and parks that come to life in summer. The people of Oslo's 'Greenwich Village' are younger and live closer together than those in the West End. Few of the inhabitants earn their living in the mills along the Akerselva River these days, and both lifestyle and architecture are more modest here. The area around St Hanshaugen consists mainly of quiet streets, apartment blocks and villas. Many come to this green haven in spring to enjoy an outdoor beer.

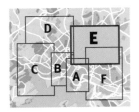

TRANCHER

BAR BOCA

RESTAURANTS

Villa Paradiso (E C3)
→ Olaf Ryes plass 8
Tel. 22 34 40 60
Mon-Fri 8am–11pm (10pm Mon); Sat-Sun 10am–11pm (10pm Sun)
Genuine Neapolitan pizza, baked in wood stoves. Playroom for children and outdoor tables giving onto Grüners gate. Pizza NOK 89–159.

Trancher (E C3)
→ Thorvald Meyers g. 78
Tel. 22 36 47 60
Daily 4–11pm
For meat-lovers as steak entrecôte is the only main on the menu. It's perfectly tenderized and previously slow-cooked in the oven for 4–6 hrs and served with a selection of side dishes. NOK 150–170.

Nighthawk Diner (E C3)
→ Seilduksg. 15a
Tel. 96 62 73 27
Mon-Fri 7–1am (2am Wed-Thu; 3am Fri); Sat-Sun 10–3am (1 am Sun)
Every single interior detail in this American diner is authentic, from the ceiling fans and juke box to the leather-clad booths and waitresses uniforms. Burger NOK 169.

Sult (E C3)
→ Thorvald Meyers g. 26
Tel. 22 87 04 67
Mon-Fri 4.30pm–1am; Sat-Sun noon–1am
Taking its name from Knut Hamsun's famous 1890 novel (Hunger in English), this restaurant offers creative, value-for-money cuisine. On Fridays, the bar, Tørst, serves free tapas, and you can eat there if Sult is full. Carte NOK 200–225.

Markveien Mat & Vinhus (E C4)
→ Torvbakkg. 12
Tel. 22 37 22 97
Mon-Sat 5pm–11pm (wine bar 4pm–1am)
Grünerløkka's classic, upscale restaurant is set in cosy rooms whose walls are hung with works of art. Main courses include wild lamb, Norwegian kid, suckling pig, veal and halibut – always fresh – which are cooked with a Mediterranean touch. Next door is Dr. Kneipp's terrific wine bar. Carte NOK 238– 294.

CAFÉS, BARS

Java espressobar (E A4)
→ Ullevålsvn. 45 B
Tel. 22 59 46 37
Mon-Sat 7am (9am Sat)–6pm; Sun 10am–5pm
People come to Java for Robert Thoresen, Barista

ETTS CAFÉ

PARKTEATRET

SHOE LOUNGE

World Champion in 2000, who still serves great espresso with creative motifs in the foam.

Bar Boca (E C3)
→ *Thorvald Meyers g. 30*
Tel. 22 04 10 80; Mon-Sat 11am–1am (3am Fri-Sat); Sun noon–1am
The best drinks in town are mixed in this little bar with oval-shaped tables and 1950s-style lamps.

Café 33 (E C3)
→ *Thorvald Meyers g. 33*
Tel. 22 38 55 15
Daily 2pm–3am
A local watering hole with an interesting generation mix. Norwegian food, good atmosphere.

Colletts Café (E A3)
→ *Colletts g. 33*
Tel. 22 60 19 20; Daily noon–midnight (1am Tue-Sat; 10pm Sun)
Spanish cuisine is served in this cosy café on St Hanshaugen.

Underwater (E A4)
→ *Dalsbergstien 4*
Tel. 22 46 05 26; Mon-Sat 4pm–3am (1am Mon-Tue); live opera Tue and Thu 9pm–12.30am
Pub with aquarium-style decor. Sopranos make the large fish tanks vibrate with live performances. Cheap beer for students on Wednesdays.

CONCERTS, THEATRES

Blå (E C3)
→ *Brenneriveien 9C; Tel. 22 20 91 81; Daily 9pm–3.30am (tables outside noon–midnight); blaaoslo.no*
Jazz, rock and electronica in an old textile mill by the Akerselva River. Blå is on *Downbeat*'s list of the world's best jazz clubs. The outdoor tables are among Oslo's most picturesque; crafts market every Sunday.

Parkteatret (E C4)
→ *Olaf Ryes plass 11*
Tel. 22 35 63 00
parkteatret.no
Theatre, rock music and literary evenings in a 250-seat hall. Stylish and popular 1930s-style bar.

Kulturslottet Soria Moria (E D1)
→ *Vogts g. 64*
Tel. 22 15 25 70; sult.no
The Torshov château has a café, cinema and the Torshovteateret: a division of the National Theatre.

Trikkestallen (E D2)
→ *Torshovgt. 33; Tel. 23 47 40 830; slonye.no*
This is the puppet-theatre side of the very popular Oslo Nye Theatre. Puppet shows for children of all ages.

Black Box (E D3)
→ *Marstrandg. 8; Tel. 23 40 77 70; blackbox.no*
Shows by independent Norwegian and foreign theatre ensembles.

SHOPPING

Markveien, Thorvald Meyers gate (E C2-4)
These two Grünerløkka avenues and their side streets are home to a myriad of small, often alternative, cafés and design shops selling clothes, jewellery, crafts and retro items. Great for vintage shopping.

Velouria Vintage (E C3)
→ *Thorvald Meyers g. 34*
Tel. 90 97 51 91; Mon-Fri 11am–7pm; Sat 11am–6 pm; Sun noon–6 pm
Cowboy boots from the American East coast, dresses and French accessories.

Shoe Lounge (E C3)
→ *Thorvald Meyers g. 42*
Tel. 22 37 50 07
Mon-Sat 11am–5pm (6pm Thu; 4pm Sat)
Shoes from Marc Jacobs, Acne, Miss Sixty, Patrizia Pepe and the house brand.

Boa (E C4)
→ *Thorvald Meyers g. 50*
Tel. 22 38 04 91; Mon-Sat 11am–6pm (5pm Sat)

Women's fashion designed by, among others, owners Mette Møller and Merete Taule.

Probat (E C4)
→ *Thorvald Meyers g. 54*
Tel. 22 35 20 70
Mon-Sat 11am–5pm
Fun, homemade T-shirts with a twist.

Day Dreams & Pearls (E C4)
→ *Markveien 34; Tel. 95 90 14 28; Tue-Sat 11am–6pm (7pm Thu; 4pm Sat)*
Pretty jewellery and accessories from the likes of Zuzanna G, who has a brand store around the corner, in Helgesens gate.

Babel (E C4)
→ *Markveien 54; Tel. 24 20 03 51; Mon-Sat 11am–5pm (6pm Thu; 4pm Sat)*
See by Chloé, Rules by Mary, James Perse T-shirts and other labels.

Brudd (E C4)
→ *Markveien 42*
Tel. 22 38 23 98; Tue-Sat 11am–5pm (4pm Sat)
Norwegian-designed glass and jewellery.

Med og uten (E C4)
→ *Korsg. 22*
Tel. 22 04 66 00; Mon-Fri 11am–6pm (5pm Mon-Tue); Sat 11am–5pm
Designer fashion for both sexes, including brands that are hard to find elsewhere in Oslo.

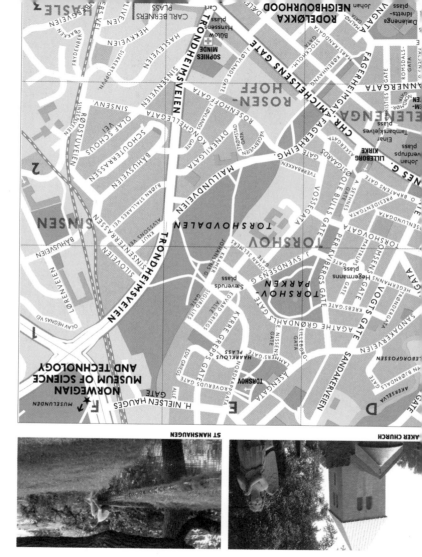

GRENSEVEIEN

0 100 200 m

▲ Map F

ELØKKA NEIGHBOURHOOD

MUSEUM OF SCIENCE AND TECHNOLOGY

D OG A – CENTRE FOR DESIGN AND ARCHITECTURE

ch has been a sacrificial , a fresh water reservoir a graveyard for horses. park, started in 1865, boasts an artificial am, a pond for the ns, sculptures, and an door restaurant by the ilion on Festplassen.

elthusbakken (E B3) e a barren no-man's- ll, Telthusbakken t Hill), was developed Oslo's poor in the late century. Since the os the tiny, attractive den houses have been ored and some of the abitants run small etable plots just ss the road.

★ Birkelunden Park (E C2)
→ *Upper Grünerløkka*
Sit down and relax in the park under the huge birch trees. Grünerløkka became part of Christiania in 1858. The square between the school (1895) to the east and the Paulus Church (1892) to the west was originally reserved as a recreational area for the workers, and is still being used that way.

★ Rodeløkka neighbourhood (E D-E 2-3)
Dean Rode had a Telemark building transported here in 1854. The wooden block sprang up in the 1860s,

about a decade before Rodeløkka was included in the city. The 137 wooden houses were listed in 1988.

★ Norwegian Museum of Science and Technology (north of **E** F1)
→ *Kjelsåsveien 143*
Tel. 22 77 90 00
June 20–Aug 20: daily 10am–6pm; otherwise Tue-Fri 9am–4pm; Sat-Mon 11am–6pm
If you are walking or biking towards the Maridalsvannet Lake, drop by the Norsk Teknisk Museum. The Teknoteket is suitable for children, and there are activities for the whole family on weekends. The museum is easily

accessible by tram, bus or train; free parking.

★ D og A – Norwegian Centre for Design and Architecture (E C4)
→ *Hausmannsg. 16*
Tel. 23 29 28 70
Daily 10am (noon Sat-Sun)–5pm (6pm Wed-Thu); usually free; doga.no
Norwegian fashion and industrial design in an old electricity transformer station, rebuilt in the Functionalist style in 2004 and awarded the National Building Prize in 2006. Today it houses Norsk Form, the Norwegian Design Council and a gourmet restaurant.

MUNCH MUSEUM

MOSQUE

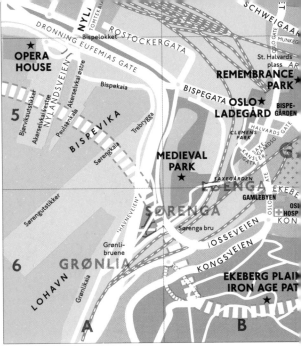

★ **Botanical Garden and Museum** (**F** B-C2-3)
→ *Sars g. 1; Tel. 22 85 17 00
Gardens: daily 7am (10am Sat-Sun)–9pm (5pm Oct-March 14; greenhouses: Tue-Sun 11am–4pm*
The Botanisk Hage og Museum is a green oasis in the middle of the asphalt jungle. Not to be missed are the Norwegian rock garden with its 1,000 plants, waterfalls and nature trails; the arboretum; the collection of aromatic plants in the scented garden (texted in Braille); and the tropical/temperate climate plants in Victoria-huset and Palmehuset.

★ **Geological Museum** (**F** C2)
→ *Sars g. 1; Tel. 22 85 17 00
Tue-Sun 11am–4pm*
Hailed as 'the missing link' between man and ape, the 47 million year-old primate fossil Ida caused a worldwide sensation when it was discovered in 2009. A full-scale skeleton of a Tyrannosaurus rex, together with gems and rocks from Norway's geological history, will also please visitors.

★ **Zoological Museum** (**F** C2)
→ *Details as above*
The Zoologisk Museum follows the evolutionary history of Norway. It is best known for the Svalbard room, which contains polar bears and arctic animals.

★ **Munch Museum** (**F** C3)
→ *Tøyeng. 53
Tel. 23 49 35 00; June-Aug: daily 10am–6pm; Sep-May: Tue-Fri 10am–4pm; Sat-Sun 11am–5pm*
The Expressionist Edvard Munch (1863–1944) is one of the few Nordic painters to have had a decisive influence on art. More than half his paintings (the most famous hang in the National Gallery (see **B**), portraits, graphic works, preserved graphic printing plates and sculptures can be seen in this museum which dates from 1963.

★ **Mosque** (**F** C4)
→ *Åkebergveien 28b
Tel. 22 68 27 08;
Visits by appt, check wim.*
Norway's first purpose-b mosque, the Central Jam Mosque, was complete 1995 and is defined by i tall minarets. Iranian m artists were brought in t decorate the prayer roo that faces Mecca. The considerable immigratio into Norway since the 1 from countries such as Turkey and Pakistan me that today a variety of muslim denominations represented in Oslo.

ZOOLOGICAL MUSEUM

GEOLOGICAL MUSEUM

BOTANICAL GARDEN
AND MUSEUM

GRØNLAND KIRKE
GRØNLAND
DET ÅPNE TEATRET
SCHWEIGAARDS
POST-TERMINALEN
Schweigaards
bru
OSLO
SENTRALSTASJON

Helga
Helg. pl.
Enerhaugs
plass

SPEKTRUM
JERNBANETORGET
Sonja Henies pl.
TORGET
Smalgangen
JERNBANE- T

ST. HALLVARD
SØRLIGATA
GRØNLAND GATE
TØYENGATA
NORDBYGATA
MOTZFELDTS GATE
URTEHAGEN
LAKKEGATA
VATERLANDS-
VATERLANDS-
BRUGATA
PARKEN
HEDMARKSGATE
HEBERGATA
VATERLAND

BOTA GÅRD MU
TØYEN KIRKE
HEIDALS GATE
UTTØYENGATA
NORBYGATA
CHRISTIAN KROHGS GATE
LANDSEN
STORGATA
HERSLEBS GATE
BERNT ANKERS GATE
CALMEYERS GATE
OSTERHAUS GATE

GAMLE FJELLHAGEN
Rudolf Nilsens
plass
BOTA GÅRD MU
VAHLS GATE
LAKKEGATA
OSLO KOMM.
SLÅMOTGANGEN
STORGATA

SARS GATE
Wexels plass
AKERSELVA
LAKKEGATA
JAKOB KIRKE
HAUSMANNS GATE
Th. Kirkelsens plass
SØNDRE GATE
LAKKEGATA
ØSTRE ELVEBAKKEN
VESTRE BAKKEN
MÆRDRES VEI
LAKKEGATA

SARS GATE
JENS BJELKES GATE
TRONDHEIMSVEIEN
SØNDRE GATE
THORVALD
LEIRFALLS-GATA
TORVBAKK-GATA
BRENNERIVEIEN

Z
SOFIENBERG
SCHLEPPEGRELLS GATE
RATHKES GATE
SOFIENBERGGATA
SOFIENBERG
HERSLEBS GATE
SVERDRUPSGATE
PROF. DAHLS GATE
KIRKEVEIEN
PAULS GATE
MEYERS GATE
NORDRE
KORSGATA
NEDRE GATE
ØVRE GATE
STOLMAKERG
Schous plass
BLYTTS

TOFTES GATE
SOFIENBERGGATA
SOFIENBERG GATE
GRÜNERHAGEN PARK
Olaf Ryes plass
MARK VEIEN

HELGESENS GATE
GÖTEBORG GATA
GRAVLUND
MOSAISK
SOFIENBERGS PARKEN
Gisle Johnsons plass
PARKTEATRET
Grüners plass
OLAF RYES GATE
MARKVEIEN
FOSSVEIEN
NEDRE FOSS
MARSELIS GATE
Grüner-brua

FELLE
FREIAPARKEN
Rødes plass
G. plass
LANG
KIRKEVEIEN
KARL STADSGATA
HELGESENS GATE
STEENSTRUPS GATE
BERGVERKS GATE
ØVRE FOSS

B
MALMÖGATA
Johan Thronos plass
Holsts plass
GØTEBORGGATA
KØBENHAVNGATA
SELDUKSGATA
GRÜNER-LØKKA
HELGESENS GATE
STEENSTRUPS GATE
MARKVEIEN
STRUBERGATA
GRÜNER

PAULUS KIRKE
HASLUNDS GATE
DALENENGA GATE
IDRETTSPLASS
Birkelunden
Paulus plass
NISSENS GATE
GRÜNER STUBBEN

Gamlebyen is a district of contrasts: pastoral medieval ruins mix with high-rise modernism and faded old buildings, while city trams and long-distance trains thunder by. Oslo's oldest area also holds the youngest, most exotic population. Grønland is full of multicultural eateries, hip bars, cafés and shops, but no polar bears – to see those, you have to go to Tøyen and the Zoological Museum. A lot of the traffic now runs through tunnels underneath the new opera house, set to be the heart of this new area, surrounded by wide avenues, parks and expensive apartments.

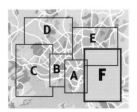

EKEBERGRESTAURANTEN

TEDDY'S SOFT BAR

RESTAURANTS

Punjab Tandoori (F B4)
→ Grønland 24; Tel. 22 17 20 86; Daily 11am–11pm
Don't let the run-down interior put you off, Kiranjot's best-selling homemade Indian tandoori chicken is incredible value for money. Tandoori dish with rice and nan NOK 70.

Vognmand Nilsen (F B4)
→ Rubina Ranas g. 3; Tel. 22 05 92 00; Daily 11.30am–midnight (Sun 2pm)
Named after one of the many Swedish immigrants who settled in Grønland a hundred years ago, Vognmand Nilsen is housed in a new minimalist building. The menu is minimalist too – but with such treats as entrecôte with bean salad, cremini mushrooms, fried parsley and rosemary glaze at NOK 145–225. Three-course menu NOK 345.

Kampen bistro (F D3)
→ Bøgata 21
Tel. 22 19 77 08; Daily 3pm (1pm Sat-Sun)–1am
A local restaurant, simply furnished with pine tables and 1950s-style lamps, and renowned for a simple, yet beautifully presented Norwegian cuisine. Jazz concerts for adults and/or children every Sunday. Meat or fish course NOK 235.

Oslo spiseforretning (F B5)
→ Oslog. 15
Tel. 22 62 62 10; Tue–Sat 4pm–midnight Outside tables May-Aug: Tue-Sun 3–10pm (Sun 1pm)
Cosy 1920s establishment where produce from small-scale Norwegian farms is prepared with gourmet zeal to spirited old-style recipes. Outside, simpler snacks are served, and on the second floor, a 1925 apartment is used as a private dining room. Carte NOK 232–289.

Ekebergrestauranten (F C3)
→ Kongsvn. 15; Tel. 23 24 23 00; Mon-Sat 11am–midnight; Sun noon–10pm
The best view in town and a modern gourmet kitchen makes this 1929 Functionalist gem a popular destination after a romantic walk from town or from Ekebergsletta. If you're not hungry, settle for a drink in the bar or snuggle up in front of the fireplace with a cocoa. Carte NOK 250–280.

GLORIA FLAMES

MADINA SWEETS

BENNY BUTIKK

CAFÉS, BARS

Evita Espressobar (F A4)
→ Smalgangen 1A
Tel. 22 17 48 89; Mon-Fri
7am–8pm; Sat-Sun 9am
(10am Sun)–7pm
The first coffee bar in
Gamlebyen, opened in
1997, serves cakes, teas,
ciabatta sandwiches and
snacks.

Teddy's Soft Bar (F A3)
→ Brugata 3A Tel. 22 17
36 00; Daily 11am–1am
(or later) (3am Fri-Sat)
The original 1958
Wurlitzer jukebox remains
intact, from the time
Teddy's introduced
milkshakes to Oslo. Take
a nostalgic trip and play
three golden oldies for
only NOK 10! Musicians
and media types admire
the authentic, well-
preserved interior of
this bar.

Oslo Mekaniske Verksted (F A3)
→ Joachim Nielsens gang
Tel. 45 23 75 34
Daily 3pm–2am
This dimly lit cave-like
bar has comfy leather
seats and tasteful pieces
of old furniture; perfect
for an afternoon reading
or chatting. Food is
also served. Beautiful
outside space.

Asylet (F B4)
→ Grønland 28; Tel. 22 17
09 39; Mon-Fri 11am–
midnight; Sat-Sun noon–
1am (11pm Sun)
This local hangout, in a
merchant building dating
from 1740, serves trout,
sandwiches and
meatballs. Cosy fireplace
in winter; in the summer,
enjoy your meal under
cherry blossoms in the
courtyard.

Dattera til Hagen (F A3)
→ Grønland 10; Tel. 22 17
18 61; Mon-Sat 11am–
midnight (2am Thu; 3am
Fri-Sat); Sun noon–
midnight; dattera.no
It has a café on the
ground floor with cosy but
slightly worn sofas, a club
on the first floor and a
pretty backyard café. DJs,
concerts or theatre
performances Tue-Sun.

Gloria Flames (F B4)
→ Grønland 18 Tel. 22 17
16 00; Mon-Sat 4pm–3am;
gloriaflames.no
Large rock bar behind an
inconspicuous façade,
with a massive sound
system. Spot the queue
of 20–30-year-olds
outside at weekends.
Pancakes on the roof in
summer and free Tuesday
concerts. The beer is
cheaper between Sunday
and Wednesday.

Olympen (F B4)
→ Grønlandsleiret 15
Tel. 24 10 19 99; Mon-Sat
11am–1am (3.30am Wed-
Sat); Sun noon–1am
Elegant beer hall with
high ceilings and
sparkling chandeliers,
cosy oak panels, tasty,
traditional food and more
than 100 types of beer.
You can stay here from
mid-morning until the
next door Pigalle night
club opens.

SHOPPING

Madina Sweets (F B3)
→ Tøyeng. 27
Tel. 22 68 48 08; Mon-Sat
10am–9pm; Sun 1–9pm
Got a craving for Asian
food? You could eat your
way from Grønlandsleiret
to Tøyengata, but make
sure you're not too full by
the time you reach
Madina Sweets, where
jalaba (deep-fried honey
bagels) and other
Pakistani delights are
beautifully displayed on
the counter. NOK 100/kg.

Mithas Sweethouse (F A3)
→ Grønland. 2b
Tel. 22 17 00 03; Mon-Sat
10am–9pm; Sun noon–8pm
Delicious Iranian cakes
and Arabic and Pakistani
sweets, fit for an Asian

wedding. Baklava NOK
100/kg (NOK 50/lb).

Saab Tekstil (F B4)
→ Smalgangen 9
Tel. 22 17 09 40; Mon-Sat
10am–7pm (6pm Sat)
Silk, brocade, cotton and
other fabrics and a large
range of shoes and
accessories. They will
also make dresses and
saris to order.

Grønland Basar (F B4)
→ Tøyengata 2
Tel. 22 17 05 71; Mon-Sat
10am–8pm (6pm Sat)
There is a distinctly
Middle Eastern
atmosphere behind the
wonderful façade of this
exotic shopping mall.
Stalls selling jewellery,
clothes, homeware and
trinkets from Turkey and
Egypt rub shoulders with
the halal butcher.

Benny Butikk fengselsutsalg (F B4)
→ Entrance to the left
of 'Egonporten'
Tel. 22 30 17 71;
Tue and Thu noon–6pm
Prices are as low as the
ceiling in Benny's
Prison's basement shop.
Sells rocking horses,
knickknacks and works
made from textiles, glass,
wrought iron and paper –
created by inmates at
local prisons. Custom
orders are also taken.

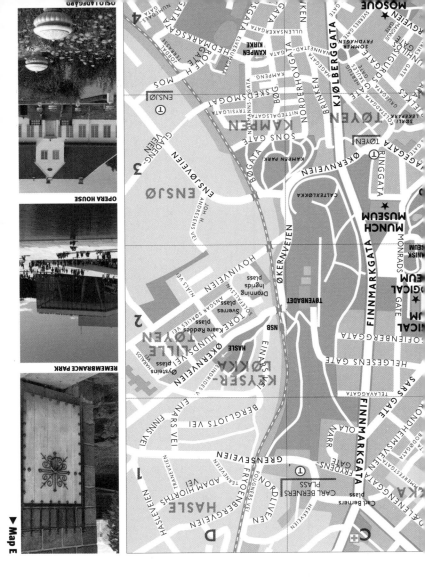

OSLO LADEGÅRD

OPERA HOUSE

REMEMBRANCE PARK

▶ Map E

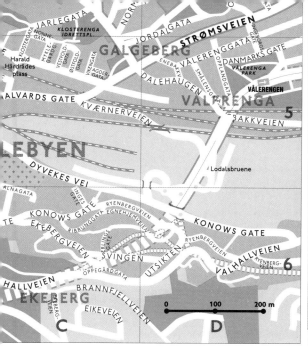

MEDIEVAL PARK

VIEW OF THE FJORD FROM THE EKEBERG PLAIN

**membrance
rk (F** B5)
St Hallvards plass, entry
Oslogate / Bispegata
nneparken and its ruins
te from the middle ages.
sest to Bispegata lie
e ruins of St Hallvard-
edralen (c.1070), which
s once the medieval
/'s cathedral, and
obably resembled Gamle
er Kirke (see **E**). There
 also ruins of
rskirken, Olavsklosteret
d Olavskirken, plus a
n-century Dominican
vent.

Oslo Ladegård (F B5)
Oslog. 13 (St Hallvards pl.)
 22 19 44 68; May 20-Sep:

medieval walks Wed 6pm and
Sun 1pm; tour of Ladegården
Sun 3pm
Built around 1720 on the
ruins of the old episcopal
residence (13th century),
Oslo Ladegård presents
models of the city structure
and burial customs from
the Middle Ages to the 17th
century in authentic 18th-
and 19th-century rooms.
Frequent concerts.

★ **Medieval Park (F** B5)
➔ Entrance at the junction
Oslog./ Saxegaards g.
Every August, the
preserved, medieval
church ruins in this park at
Sørenga come to life during
the Øya festival (Oslo's

biggest rock festival). The
artificial lake Vannspeilet
shows the water level as it
was in medieval times.

★ **Ekeberg Plain /
Iron-Age path** (**F** B6)
Ekebergsletta and
Jernalderstien incorporates
Oslo's biggest park, which,
every year, hosts one of the
world's largest youth
football tournaments – the
Norway Cup. The park was
established in 1947. A zoo,
horseback riding, outdoor
café and mini golf make for
a perfect day out. Also, 65
grave mounds and the
city's oldest rock carvings
(4,000–5,000 years old)
from the Iron Age. An Iron-

Age trail leaves from
Karlsborgveien.

★ **Opera House (F** A5)
➔ Kirsten Flagstad plass 1
Tel. 21 42 21 00 (box office:
815 444 88); Mon-Sat 10am–
11pm (11am Sat); Sun noon–
midnight; operaen.no
The Norwegian Opera and
Ballet opened in April 2008
and is Oslo's newest
landmark. You can walk on
the sloping roof and enjoy
the views of the city, but
take your sunglasses as
the brightness of the white
marble is blinding! The
main auditorium seats
1,364, while the two other
stages seat up to 440 and
200 people.

GARDERMOEN AIRPORT

METRO SIGN

OSLO TRAM

Spend the night by the Maridalsvannet Lake and enjoy the lovely scenery. NOK 459–660.

NOK 500–1,000

Budget Hotel (**A** C4)
→ *Prinsens g. 6; Tel. 22 41 36 10; budgethotel.no*
A B&B right around the corner from Oslo S. Simple but clean rooms. NOK 699.

Cochs pensjonat (**B** C2)
→ *Parkv. 25; Tel. 23 33 24 00 cochspensjonat.no*
Traditional, airy night stop by the Palace Park and Hegdehaugsveien. Started by the Coch sisters in 1927 and immortalised in the novel *The Half Brother* by Norwegian writer Lars Saabye Christensen (b. 1953). NOK 770.

Perminalen (**A** B4)
→ *Øvre Slottsgate 2 Tel. 23 09 30 81 perminalen.no*
A former soldiers' hostel

close to the parliament. 55 rooms with TV, shower and desk. NOK 370/person for four sharing; double room NOK 840.

P-Hotels Oslo (**A** B3)
→ *Grensen 19 Tel. 23 31 80 00; p-hotels.no*
A cut-price chain may have taken over the former hotel Norrøna but some of the 93 rooms in this 1900 building still have a traditional cachet. No mini-bar but modern bathrooms. Breakfast tray delivered to the room. Very centrally located, close to Karl Johans Gate. NOK 995.

NOK 1,000–1,700

B&B Villa Frogner (**C** D2)
→ *Nordraaks g. 26; Tel. 22 56 19 60; bedandbreakfast.no*
Small B&B in an elegant white villa, two minutes walk from Frognerparken. Cosy rooms and garden. NOK 1,095.

Hotel Spectrum (**F** A3)
→ *Brug. 7; Tel. 23 36 27 00 thonhotels.no/spectrum*
Homely inn, in the east central area, between Storgata and Grønland. No restaurant, but lots of choice for low-budget meals in the area. 151 rooms. NOK 1,175.

Bondeheimen (**A** B3)
→ *Rosenkrantz' g. 8 Tel. 23 21 41 00 bondeheimen.com*
Located only 150 metres from Karl Johan, the Bondeheimen retains a distinctly Norwegian flavour. The 127 rooms have been renovated with traditional oak furniture (and equipped with Internet access). NOK 1,485.

West Hotel (**C** D3)
→ *Skovn. 15; Tel. 22 54 21 60; bestwestern.com*
A three-star hotel in the classy Frogner neighbourhood. Pets

TAXIS

When the light on the roof is lit, the taxi is available. Grab one at the nearest taxi stop, hail one in the street or book by phone.
→ *Oslo Taxi: Tel. 02323*
→ *Norges Taxi: Tel. 08000*
→ *Taxi2: Tel. 02202*

CAR

Parking in town can be a hassle; car parks in the shopping areas tend to cost slightly more.
Speed limits
→ *80–100 km (50–60 mi) / hr on country roads; 30 km (18 mi) / hr in the centre*
Car rental
Expensive. Some companies deliver and pick up at the airport, and in town.
→ *Holiday: Tel. 22 33 74 00*
→ *Avis: Tel. 815 33 044*
→ *Hertz: Tel. 22 10 00 00*

BICYCLE

In summer, practical in the centre, ideal in the Nordmarka forest. Map of bike trails for both locations are available from the tourist centres.
Rental
→ *AS Skiservice (by Voksenkollen metro station); Tel. 22 13 95 00*

AIRPORTS

**Olso Airport
Gardermoen (OSL)**
→ 48 km (30 mi) northeast
of Oslo; osl.no
Oslo's main airport.
Links to city centre
By Flytoget (express train)
→ 19–22 mins, NOK 170
By local train
→ 26 mins, NOK 110
By airport shuttle bus
→ 50 mins, NOK 140
By taxi
→ 45 mins, fixed price NOK
500–999, tel. 02323
Torp (Sandefjord)
→ 123 km (76 mi) south of
Oslo; torp.no
Rygge (Moss)
→ 60 km (37 mi) southeast
of Oslo; ryg.no

OSLO AIRPORTS

TRAINS

Oslo S (A D4)
→ Jernbanetorget
Daily 8am–11pm
Oslo Sentralstasjon
(central station) lies at
the east end of Oslo's
main street, Karl Johan.
From here, local trains
from the NSB rail
company leave for the
suburbs, for towns
around Oslo and for
Gardermoen Airport. It is
here, too, that you can
catch long-distance
trains to other cities in
Norway, Sweden and
abroad.
Information and tickets
→ Tel. 815 00 888
Daily 6am–9pm; nsb.no

• Most of Oslo's hotels are in
the central or west central
area. They rely on business
guests for their survival,
which means lower prices in
summer and at weekends,
though not as low as the
city's 14 B&Bs
• B&B prices are an
indication only – call to
discuss
• Camping, in Oslo's
beautiful suroundings, is by
far the cheapest option
• Places without a map
reference can be found on
one of two maps in the
Welcome section

PRIVATE
ACCOMMODATION

OsloVisit booking (A D4)
→ Oslo S; Tel. 815 33 0555
**Useit – The Youth
Information** (A C3)
→ Møllerg. 3; Tel. 22 41 51 32
These two companies
arrange for
accommodation in private

homes. Prices start at NOK
200 per person (bring a
sleeping bag), and NOK
560 for a double room.

CAMPING

Langøyene Camping
→ Boat 94 from Vippetangen
Tel. Friluftsetaten 02 180
Fjord enthusiasts and salt-
water worshippers can
camp two nights for free
before asking for
permission. Do check the
schedule for the boat back
to town – taxi-boats are
expensive.
Ekeberg Camping (F B6)
→ Ekebergveien 65
Tel. 22 19 85 68
ekebergcamping.no
Camping with a view!
Oslo at your feet, yet
within walking distance.
Tent/car for four: NOK 260.
**Bogstad Camp og
Turistsenter**
→ Ankerveien 117
Tel. 22 51 08 00

Forest camping by Bogstad
Lake in the Nordmarka
Forest (30 mins by bus 32
from Oslo S or
Nationaltheatret). Tent for
two people: NOK 180;
cabin sleeping four with TV
and bath: NOK 480–1285.

HOSTELS

They offer dormitories,
single or double rooms of
a decent standard. Prices
are a little higher if you are
not a member of
Norwegian Hostels or
Hostelling International.
→ Tel. 23 12 45 10
hostels.no
Anker Hostel (F A3)
→ Storg. 55; Tel. 22 99 72 00
Central location by
Grünerløkka and the
Akerselva River, only 10
minutes from the city
centre. Breakfast is served
6–11.30am, but you can
hire kitchenware and cook
your own breakfast in the

kitchen. Double room NOK
560; dormitory NOK 200.
Bring your own bed linen
or hire for NOK 45.
**Oslo Vandrerhjem
Haraldsheim**
(north of E F1)
→ Haraldsheimv. 4
Tel. 22 22 29 65
Nice hostel outside the
centre (metro 4 or 6 to
Sinsenkrysset). From NOK
245 in a room sleeping
four; NOK 540 for a double
room, breakfast included
Bed linen, NOK 50 extra.
**Oslo Vandrerhjem
Holtekilen**
→ Michelets v. 55; 8 km (5 mi)
west of Oslo along the E18
(bus to Sandvika, stop at
Kveldsrovn.); Tel. 67 1 80 40
Same prices as
Haraldsheim.
**Oslo Hostel Rønningen
YMCA** (B C2)
→ Myrerskogv. 54
Bus nos 55 or 56 from Storo
Tel. 21 02 36 00
Open June 1–Aug 19

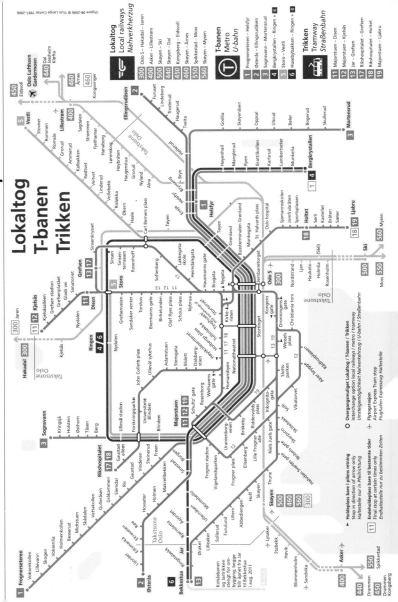

Street names and places to visit are listed alphabetically. They are followed by a map reference of which the initial letter in bold (**A**, **B**, **C**..) relates to the district and matching map.

SLO S

SLO BUS

TRAFIKANTEN

ictoria Hotel (A B3)
➤ Rosenkrantz' gate 13
el. 24 14 70 00
ca-hotels.com
legant business hotel in
ne of Oslo's busiest
treets, close to the town
all and Aker Brygge.
leasant, comfortable
ooms. Lovely high ceilings
n the breakfast hall.
OK 2,095.

Hotel Cecil (A B3)
➤ Stortingsgaten 8; Tel. 23 31
8 00; thonhotels.com/cecil
. modern hotel with
ree coffee and evening
nacks in the breakfast
oom. NOK 2,195.

laza Hotel (F A4)
➤ Sonja Henies pl. 3
el. 22 05 80 00; radissonblu.
om/plazahotel-oslo
. five-star, high-rise glass
nonument with 650
ooms and 23 suites,
merald green carpets and
ream-coloured walls.
itness room, baby-sitting

service, Oslo's highest
bar, several restaurants,
swimming pool and more.
NOK 2,195.

Scandinavia Hotel (B D2)
➤ Holbergs g. 30
Tel. 23 29 30 00; radissonblu.
com/scandinaviahotel-oslo
The 'SAS hotel' is best
known for the panoramic
views from the Summit 21
bar. 491 rooms in Art Deco,
Oriental, Italian, Nordic or
Continental styles – or just
business class, with a little
extra luxury thrown in.
NOK 2,195.

Hotel Bristol (A B2)
➤ Kristian IVs g. 7
Tel. 22 82 60 00
thonhotels.no/bristol
One of Oslo's historic
hotels, by the National
Gallery. The 252 rooms are
well appointed. Together
with the Bristol Grill, the
Library Bar and the Winter
Garden, they exude a
certain English charm.
NOK 2,295.

LUXURY HOTELS

Grand Hotel (A B3)
➤ Karl Johans g. 31
Tel. 23 21 20 00; grand.no
Each day at noon, Henrik
Ibsen drank his coffee in
the hotel's Grand Café. In
summer and at weekends,
prices may drop low
enough to enable mere
mortals to mingle with the
international stars and the
heads of state who stay
here. NOK 2,645.

Hotel Continental (A A3)
➤ Stortingsg. 24–26
Tel. 22 82 40 00
hotel-continental.no
Ranked as one of the best
hotels in the world, with a
splendid Art Deco façade,
it is perfectly located by
the National Theatre. The
rooms were recently
renovated. Excellent
restaurant, Theatercaféen.
Legendary breakfast
buffet. Faultless service.
NOK 2,835.

PUBLIC TRANSPORT

Ruter AS runs the
city's six metro lines,
six tramway lines and
50 bus lines.
Information
➤ Trafikanten,
Jernbanetorget 1; Tel. 177
Mon-Fri 7am–11pm;
Sat-Sun 8am–11pm
Fares
➤ Single ticket: NOK 26
(pre bought from kiosks)
NOK 40 (from the driver)
➤ Flexi card (eight
journeys): NOK 190
➤ One-day card: NOK 70
➤ One-week card:
NOK 210
Metro (T-bane)
The best means of
transport if you need to
get to the suburbs.
Electric tram (trikk)
Runs in the inner city,
and is a good way of
exploring the streets.
Bus
Ideal in areas that
are not accessible by
tram or metro, such as
Bygdøy for example.
Night buses
➤ Sat-Sun 1–4am
Normal fare.
Boats
Vippetangen to
Hovedøya & Langøyene
➤ Line 94 from
Vippetangen (**A** B6).
Rådhusbrygge 3-
Bygdøy (**B** C-D5)
➤ Line 91 (April-Sep only)
You can use standard
public transport tickets.
Leaving the city
Ruter AS buses go to
the Akershus county,
around Oslo.
Information
➤ Bussterminalen (Coach
station **F** A4), Galleri Oslo,
Grønland; Tel. 23 00 24 00

OSLO'S MAIN ROADS

OSLO PASS

This pass allows unlimited travel by tram, bus, metro, train and boat. It also entitles the holder to free entry to all the big museums and outdoor pools; reduced prices for boat trips; for car, ski and skate rental; theatre tickets; and the right to park in municipal parking spaces.

- 24 hrs: NOK 230 (children NOK 100)
- 48 hrs: NOK 340 (children NOK 120)
- 72 hrs: NOK 430 (children NOK 160)

→ *The pass is free if you buy the Oslo Package, see visitoslo.com*

welcome. 8 of the 56 rooms have balconies. NOK 1,595.

Holmenkollen Park Hotel

→ *Kongeveien 26; 15 minutes walk from Holmenkollen metro statio (line 1) Tel. 22 92 20 00 holmenkollenparkhotel.no*

A stunning 1894 wood hotel, built in the national romantic style, with gables, turrets and odd juts. The gourmet restaurant De Fem Stuer and the proximity to walking- and skiing tracks and the Holmenkollen ski jump make this an ideal place to stay for gourmet ski enthusiasts. NOK 1,600.

Hotel Gyldenløve (D E4)

→ *Bogstadv. 20 Tel. 23 33 23 00 thonhotels.com/gyldenlove*

A modern hotel with urban minimalist design, within walking distance of the Colosseum cinema,

Frognerparken and some of Oslo's most sophisticated fashion shops. NOK 1,625.

Karl Johan Hotel (A B3)

→ *Karl Johans g. 33 Tel. 23 16 17 00; karljohan.no*

Elegant hotel dating from 1899 with a striking façade giving onto Oslo's main street. Thick carpets and marble in the reception area, but plain rooms, the quietest of which are at the back. NOK 1,695.

NOK 1,700–1,900

Hotel Bastion (A C5)

→ *Skipperg. 7 Tel. 22 47 77 00; hotelbastion.no*

Behind the modern façade of this building by the Astrup Fearnley Museum is this very stylish hotel. Tastefully decorated rooms and friendly service. A corner of luxury in the Kvadraturen. NOK 1,700.

Gabelshus Hotel (C D4)

→ *Gabels g. 16; Tel. 23 27 65 00; choicehotels.no*

A charming, ivy-covered hotel close to Bygdøy Allé, where free evening meals are served in the cosy living rooms. If you're suddenly hungry you can make your own waffles in the dining room. Spa in the basement. NOK 1,880.

Hotel Savoy (A B2)

→ *Universitetsg. 11; Tel . 23 35 42 00; choicehotels.no*

This classic Oslo hotel from 1916, close to the National Gallery and the Historical Museum, has been entirely renovated in recent years. The former English hotel bar has also been updated to match the style of Savoy's new gourmet restaurant, Eik. NOK 1,930.

Hotel Royal Christiania (A D3)

→ *Biskop Gunnerus' g. 3 Tel. 23 10 80 00*

clarionroyalchristiania.no Norway's best business hotel has 508 simple rooms just outside Oslo S. NOK 1,945.

Grims Grenka (A B4)

→ *Kongens gate 5 Tel.23 10 72 00 firsthotels.com*

Luxury design hotel with spacious rooms – the largest ones are over 70 sq. m (750 sq. ft) – all tastefully decorated. Very comfortable throughout, with cocktail bar and a rooftop lounge. NOK 2,665. Standard room NOK 1,995.

OVER NOK 2,000

Hotel Opera (A D5)

→ *Christian Frederiks pl. 5 Tel. 24 10 30 00 thonhotels.com/opera*

Some of the 434 light but small rooms afford great views of the fjord and Oslo Opera House. NOK 2,070.